Praise
PUBLIC TRUST BETRAYED

"Appraisal issues played a major role in the housing boom and bust. To get an insider's view of that historic and horrendous cycle—and the troubling reality of where we are now—read this book."

—Kenneth Harney, Syndicated Columnist,
Washington Post Writers Group

"This is one man's story about the deceptions he saw in the home appraisal market, deceiving homeowners and lenders alike. It will open your eyes."

—Jane Bryant Quinn,
author of Making the Most of Your Money NOW

"Great read for anyone involved in housing finance. Understanding the foundation, which has always been valuation of the underlying collateral, and how eroded it's become should be of concern to all of us. A new and truly independent regulatory model is needed now more than ever to level the playing field and re-establish the prestige the appraisal industry once held before automation and the contradictory interests of realtors, builders and lenders destroy it all together."

—Aaron Krowne,
Founder of Implode-O-Meter

"With insight born from experience, Manning sheds light on the need for greater transparency in our country's real estate appraisal industry. The objective, independent property appraisal can no longer be taken for granted. Anyone who has ever bought or sold real estate—or plans to in the future—should read this book."

—-Keith Waddell, President and CFO,
Fortune 1000 professional services firm

PUBLIC TRUST
BETRAYED

MAY 14, 2011

Best wishes –

[signature]

James E. Manning

PUBLIC TRUST

BETRAYED

The Truth Behind
The Real Estate
Appraisal Industry

TATE PUBLISHING & Enterprises

Published by Tate Publishing & Enterprises, LLC
127 E. Trade Center Terrace | Mustang, Oklahoma 73064 USA
1.888.361.9473 | www.tatepublishing.com

Tate Publishing is committed to excellence in the publishing industry. The company reflects the philosophy established by the founders, based on Psalm 68:11,
"The Lord gave the word and great was the company of those who published it."

Published in the United States of America

ISBN: 978-1-61739-367-9
Business & Economics, Real Estate
10.09.09

Dedication

I would like to dedicate this book to all of the thousands of hard-working, honest, and ethical appraisers all over this country that have had to watch, in horror, their careers and businesses evaporate because of the greed and bad judgment of others over the past few years, but who have still managed to stand their ground and do the "Right Thing" in the face of adversity.

Acknowledgments

I want to thank my wife Shely for standing by my side, especially during the past five years, when my whole appraisal world was imploding, and giving me the courage to always believe in myself, my God, and my family around me.

I want to thank Dr. Ron Lawrence for showing me the way to re-creation, believing in me when I didn't even believe in myself, and most importantly, teaching me to see the best in people and not just the worst; from the sales clerk to the most powerful politician, we are all in this together!

I want to thank all of those men and women who post on Appraisersforum.com who oftentimes gave me the incentive and drive to keep going with this project by writing about the day-to-day occurrences in their appraisal lives and sharing their personal opinions and comments about the appraisal industry. They were all a constant source of both inspiration and frustration.

Aaron Krowne's Implode-O-Meter was also a great source of inspiration and information as it covered the lender implosion like no other media source. Its day-to-day coverage was (and still is) like a never-ending soap opera based on mortgage and lending entities and their activities.

I want to thank Pamela Crowley and George Dodd for their tireless efforts when it came to the appraisal industry and their Dodd/Crowley IVPI Proposal to change the industry for the better.

Table of Contents

Foreword

I had the pleasure of meeting Mr. Manning approximately eight years ago, when my wife, Eleanor, and I purchased a second home in the beautiful coastal town of Half Moon Bay in Northern California. The new home was situated directly across the street from the Manning's residence and we quickly became good friends. We often visit Half Moon Bay and no monthly stay would be complete without including Jim and Shely Manning in our dinner and vacation plans.

As I became friends with Mr. Manning, I came to appreciate his no-nonsense approach to life and his astute views of current events and, in particular, financial markets. He would explain to me how the mortgage markets had evolved, who the key players were, what the markets were doing, and how it compared to previous markets in various time-lines. He would explain how the easing of the credit standards could result in nothing short of financial Armageddon, how so many people were being led to the slaughter with the "Option Payment ARM," how millions of home-buyers were bidding up the prices of local real estate (oftentimes without using any of their own money), and the list goes on. All of this was years before I read, or heard of, the worldwide recession or "credit crunch" we have recently experienced.

In fact, Mr. Manning had become so alarmed at what was happening around him that he quietly took his daughter's college money and his IRA retirement funds and transferred them into US treasuries as the stock market approached 14,000 on the Dow. Talk about timing!

I never appreciated the role of the appraiser in the grand scheme of things. This has changed over the years as Mr. Manning has shared his insights with me on many occasions. His observations and comments always have a ring of "good old horse sense." He is also a man of integrity and strong character, as evidenced by the numerous stories of his dealings with the shady characters of the mortgage and real estate industry.

This book is an absolute "must read" for anyone with a financial stake in our economic and financial future. Most of what Mr. Manning describes is happening "under the radar" and it is imperative that this dysfunction in the mortgage markets be addressed and exposed to the public as soon as possible.

I am alarmed by the threat of extinction of the appraisal industry that Mr. Manning so clearly points out. I worry about my children and their children when it comes to the future of our financial markets, our real estate markets, and the growing sense of entitlement and greed that our younger generations are displaying. I, like Mr. Manning, sincerely hope that regulators, lenders, politicians, and all key players come to their senses in respect to fixing the problem of valuations in the mortgage industry.

—Ronald Lawrence MD, M.Sc., Ph.D.
Malibu, CA
Former Clinical Professor,
UCLA School of Medicine

Sifting Through the Rubble

One of the most important components of the lending industry, the appraisal, is under siege and may well become extinct in the next few years, or sooner, if steps to head off the catastrophe are not implemented. This could further delay our economic recovery and prevent easy access to mortgage capital needed for any sort of rebound in housing prices. Furthermore, it puts at risk the transparency and credibility of the valuations of the underlying assets securing trillions of dollars worth of mortgage-back securities, bonds, various derivatives, and financial instruments that our pension funds, mutual funds, retirement accounts, municipalities, universities, and others have invested in over the past thirty years.

I have seen my chosen career decimated during the past ten years by the greed and stupidity of people who are supposedly a lot brighter than I am. I am not only talking about bankers, real estate agents, loan brokers, and Wall Street types, but also about credit rating firm analysts, loan underwriters, and mortgage borrowers/real estate purchasers, all of whom helped fuel the fire of price appreciation.

The warning signs were everywhere, but were widely ignored by most. In fact, most of the appraisers that were employed by World Savings as staff appraisers supervising me and other WIC's (World Independent Contractors) had never been through a complete real estate cycle, which normally lasted eight to twelve years. They were convinced that they could weather any storm because they had done it during the last downturn in the 1990s. They reminded us often of how they performed better than most other lending institutions during that era because of their appraisal department, appraisal knowledge, and because of their emphasis on the valuation process when underwriting a loan over other aspects of the loan requirements. It might have worked in the 1990s, but coupled with their "Option Payment ARM" loan, this combination was deadly. As you probably know, World Savings (Golden West Financial) was sold to Wachovia Bank, which was, in turn, taken over by Wells Fargo at the end of 2008, at the prompting of the US government to head off a potential failure.

Foreclosures are now commonplace and we are suffering the hangover from the greatest run-up of real estate values we have ever seen. Borrowers and investors, upsidedown on their mortgages, are throwing the keys of the properties to the lenders in record numbers. There is no moral obligation to keep making the mortgage payment like in the past. Nowadays, it all boils down to an economic decision.

It always struck me as odd the way Deeds of Trust (mortgages) were set up here in California. The official description was, "A promissory note secured by a deed of trust"—a promise to pay. It was almost like the way my dad described the old days. "You were only as good as your word," he used to say, and he meant it. He described the time he offered to purchase a sawmill in Oregon from this little old man in the 1940s. They agreed on a price and had an oral agreement to conclude the transaction. When my father returned with the funds from the bank, the old man hesitated, indicating that he now believed he had sold the mill too cheaply. My father reminded him that they had an oral agreement and that he gave his word. The old man spit into the spittoon and told my father that he was right, that he had given his word and he would honor the agreement.

My dad also described the Great Depression, having lived through it, and explained that what we needed was another one to level the playing field. I think he felt a depression would make people value the dollar more and not be so frivolous with their spending and borrowing habits. He used to acknowledge how tough things were during that period, but also admitted that this era gave him some of his fondest memories. These discussions I had with my father about the Great Depression were in the early 1980s.

I have been a real estate appraiser for over thirty-five years. I don't think most people appreciate the position we are in as appraisers. If you look at the typical real estate loan transaction, everybody has a stake in the transaction closing: the selling real estate broker, the listing broker, the seller, the buyer, the local title company, the termite company, the mortgage broker, the wholesale lender, and the wholesale lender representative. It will most likely include a Wall Street firm that securitizes the mortgage into mortgage-backed securities, another firm that slices the securities and bonds into tranches of various risk and then sells them to investors world-wide, and then there is the credit rating agency that gives these instruments their seal of approval.

Most of these fees are contingent on the transaction actually coming to a close. One of the few parties in this whole line-up who does not get paid based on whether the transaction closes or not, is at the absolute bottom of the totem pole, and gets paid the least amount of compensation, is the appraiser.

In fact, it is illegal for a real estate appraiser to base his or her fee on the final opinion of value. While all of the above parties earn a substantial commission based on the sales price or transaction value, the appraiser does not. That also means that all parties but the appraiser receive built-in raises as the total value of the properties and loans rise during price escalations.

The real pressure for appraisers comes from every interested party in the transaction encouraging the appraiser to "hit the number" so that the deal will close and all of those commissions will be paid. The seller does not want to take less for the property. The buyer does not want to have to come up with more down payment should the appraisal come in low. Both the real estate agents and the loan agents want their commissions and the appraiser wants to continue to perform appraisals for the mortgage broker or lender, thereby providing for his family.

This is a tremendous amount of pressure to place on one person where hundreds of thousands of dollars, maybe even millions of dollars, are involved. This pressure is compounded by the banking industry's attempt to control the appraisal process by lowering fees that it pays appraisers and controlling workflow through AMC's (Appraisal Management Companies) that the banks either own, in part or whole, or AMCs that they have become cozy with. Generally, up until a year or two ago, the fees that appraisers charge had remained at the same level for a decade or so. Keep in mind that the appraisal profession is the *only* party to the transaction that is supposed to be unbiased and totally objective! Now with the AMCs in control of the process, the fees paid to the appraiser have actually gone down, in most cases, by up to fifty percent lower than they were making just a few years ago. The other fifty percent is going to the AMCs. What profession do you know where their fees have remained flat for ten years or have gone down? Attorneys? Accountants? Real estate brokers? Loan agents?

The AMCs have their arguments in order to defend their existence. But what they don't acknowledge (or maybe don't realize) is that they are putting the most experienced and educated experts of real property valuation at risk of extinction. This business model might work for the AMC, but it does not work for the appraiser that is out in the field performing the work. How does the lending community expect an individual to acquire the necessary education and experience to become licensed, stay current with the ever-changing laws and regulations, and get re-certified every two to four years for only half of what they were making on each assignment during the past decade?

This AMC business model has not only added a profit center to banks and title provider services at the expense of putting well-trained and experienced appraisers out of business, but it allows the lenders and banks to "control" the appraisal process by controlling who is on the appraiser panel of the AMC in the first place.

The AMC model attracts appraisers who will work for minimal fees, travel outside a reasonable distance from their office or home to appraise in market areas outside their expertise, and perform appraisals within timeframes that do not allow proper analysis and documentation. I think most borrowers would be amazed at how little the appraiser who performed the appraisal on their home was actually paid by the AMC, which collected the entire $400–500.00 appraisal fee.

There is nothing objective or "arms' length" about this process. I understand that the whole idea behind the implementation of the HVCC (Home Valuation Code of Conduct, implemented May 1, 2009) was to get the appraisal ordering process out of the hands of the mortgage brokers, who, since 2000, had increased their portion of the "loan-origination pie" to over 70 percent of the total loans originated.

One of the most dangerous aspects of this whole change in the valuation industry is the lack of transparency and creditability of the appraisal report itself. As more and more critics of the HVCC come forward and voice their concerns, the reports themselves become more and more suspect because of the ineptness and inexperience of the appraiser performing the appraisal.

It is absolutely essential that the valuation of the underlying asset securing the loan be competently prepared in order for the system to work. After the credit crunch we have experienced over the past few years, it is imperative that we restore confidence and transparency to the credit markets, and that includes the mortgage securitization markets, if we are to ever have a viable market for mortgages and a healthy housing market.

"Why is this important to me and why should I care?" you may ask. Because both housing and the mortgage markets affect everybody, at every income level, whether they rent or have purchased a home. They affect interest rates on credit cards, car loans, and the interest rates you receive on savings accounts. Your pension or retirement funds invest in mortgage-backed securities, REIT's (Real Estate Investment Trusts), commercial and industrial real estate direct, derivatives, credit-default swaps, or any combination of some or all of these mentioned. Underneath most of it is a real estate appraisal that determines the value of the collateral that supports all of these financial instruments. And you want to farm these services out to the cheapest, quickest, and most inexperienced person you can find?

The damage done to housing and credit markets over the past ten years is enormous and it will take more than a few quick fixes, mergers, and government bailouts to repair. It will take a new way of dealing with the many facets of housing, banking, and regulation for the real estate markets to ever return to some sort of normalcy. We might be well served go back historically to look for guidance and inspiration in dealing with these issues. The AMCs are marketing their products based on how quickly the reports are finished, but it is far more important and prudent that the time necessary to complete a valid valuation be spent over a hastily-completed appraisal assignment.

I recently read an article in the New York Times about food inspectors hired by various food suppliers and processors who were not given enough time to complete their work in a competent manner and were only paid a fraction of what normal inspection fees might be ($1,000 instead of the typical $8,000). The result? Bacteria, such as salmonella and e.coli, were missed at a number of plants, resulting in the contamination of several food products and the infection of several hundred people.

Another story that struck me was the hiring of airline pilots and first officers, by small commuter airlines, who didn't have enough experience to be employed by the larger carriers. One first officer, in particular, flew 3,000 miles from her home in Washington State to the New Jersey area to fly a commuter route to Buffalo, only to crash into a residential neighborhood. Her approximate annual income was $20,000 to $25,000, or roughly less than half of that of a first officer at a major airline. She had roughly one-tenth of the experience that a first officer would have at a major airline. "You get what you pay for" was never more evident.

The reality is that I really don't expect the appraisal industry to survive in any meaningful way. That saddens me, not only because it is the end of my career and the end to so many careers, but because all that so many of us wanted to do was a good, honest job of valuing real estate. For years, most of us were able to stand up to special interests and shady tactics and feel good about ourselves, knowing that greed was not a factor and that when "push came to shove," we would stand our ground and not cave in. We were a proud bunch, who continued to educate ourselves and carry on the job without compromising our ethics.

We faced the harsh reality of fancy computer models called AVMs, the real estate industry's BPOs (broker property opinions), Zillow.com, and AMCs. Yet, all we ever wanted was to protect the public trust by performing honestly and independently. In the end, the bad guy won, even though the final outcome has yet to play itself out. The greed and special interest is still out there, lurking. There is simply too much money at stake for the participants to do the right thing. This is a really sad commentary on how our society has evolved.

How It All Started

I was in my early twenties in 1973, and began working for a mortgage banker by the name of The Colwell Company in Los Angeles. It was listed on the American Stock Exchange and was situated on the seventh through the eleventh floors of a skyscraper, located off Wilshire Blvd., that was once owned by Herb Alpert of The Tijuana Brass fame. This was my second job working for a large corporation, the first being for Bank of America, where I was employed as a clerk in their BankAmericard Center in Pasadena, California, where I grew up.

I landed the job at The Colwell Company the usual way: nepotism. I had been dating a girl named Suzie for a couple of years when her brother-in-law, Gary M., approached me about working for him at this mortgage company. Being extremely ambitious at the time, I jumped at the chance. I started my real estate career as a construction inspector, inspecting job sites for progress to enable Gary to make construction disbursements to contractors. This was a job that kept me outdoors the majority of the day and I found that it agreed with me. I would start my day in the office and return at the end of the day. I would use Gary's company car to carry out my duties and life seemed good. I was making more than I did at the bank, which was normal, as banks had a terrible reputation for low pay, even in those days.

As I would perform my duties every day in the office, I kept noticing these two young men who would show up each morning but leave before I would. What struck me about these two individuals were their suntans and the fact that I never saw them at the end of the day.

One day, I asked Gary who these two young men were and also asked what they did. Gary told me that they were real estate appraisers. I was twenty-one years old and very impressionable. "What's an appraiser?" I asked. Gary explained to me that these two employees went out and valued the property that was going to be used as collateral for the home improvement loans that we were making. It was also explained to me that they both had company cars, their gas was paid for (as well as their insurance), and that when their workday was over, they didn't have to come back into the office, but simply got to go home. This helped explain the suntans.

Like I said, I was impressionable and I did love the beach. I began to get chummy with one of the appraisers. I found out that one of them had a ski condo at Mammoth Mountain, a ski resort north of Los Angeles on Highway 395. They both lived at the beach. This was it! I wanted to be an appraiser. *But how?* I wondered. I soon asked Gary how I could achieve this noble goal of mine. He suggested that I take some classes in real estate appraisal at a local community college, at night. What a great idea!

I signed up immediately at Pasadena City College and attended a class in residential real estate appraisal. I remember the teacher was a practicing appraiser who liked to remind us constantly about his appraisal acumen, especially his ability to appraise citrus properties. This was a class that lasted all semester and was capped by a final exam and a written narrative appraisal report based on a residence of our choosing that we had all worked on for months. I decided to appraise Gary's house and was excited by the whole process.

Meanwhile, one of the appraisers back at the office had been fired. It was all pretty "hush-hush," but I was able to learn that he had done something unethical and was terminated. This made an opening for another appraiser, but my dreams were quickly dashed as management hired another, more seasoned appraiser to replace the fired employee. His name was James Z. and I remember being very disappointed with this turn of events. I soon began taking more classes and going to school three nights a week. I studied appraising income property, the legal aspects of real estate, real estate finance, real estate principles, real estate brokerage- any and all real estate classes I could find. I even approached the remaining sun-tanned appraiser about going out on appraisal assignments with him on my own time, which he allowed me to do. I was ready to become an appraiser!

All of this preparation paid off one day when my sun-tanned friend was abruptly fired, just like the ski bum. Again, it was hush-hush- barely a word. Here today, gone tomorrow. I was not going to let this opportunity get by me again. Gary told me I should approach the boss. Ouch … the Boss? I had never done that before and it scared me. The boss was a man named Dick H. "Mr. H.," as he was called, was short in stature and employees always said he suffered from a Napoleon complex. He was sometimes referred to as "Little Caesar," although never to his face. Mr. H. made quite an impression on me while I worked for The Colwell Company. He would walk through the offices with such authority and a sense of command; he would make you shake with his sense of power. He was truly the "Boss."

The fact that I was intimidated by Mr. H. made it all the more difficult to make an appointment for a meeting with him about hiring me as an appraiser. I wished there was another way, but I couldn't let this opportunity slip through my fingers again. I remember sitting in front of his huge desk with Mr. H. sitting behind it. He listened to my pitch and simply asked why he should give me the chance. I told him about all of the classes I had taken and the time I had spent out in the field with the other appraiser. It didn't take him long to make his decision. Yes, I would be hired as an appraiser. One thing he said to me I will never forget. He told me I now have a lot of responsibility, a lot of people are predicating career-making decisions based on my analysis and that I had better, "Keep my nose clean." That made quite an impression on me and still does to this day.

Soon, I was paired up with Jim Z. (the new appraiser), who would train me and become my mentor. I received my new company car, a Ford Torino, that would prove to be not only economical (with the use of a company gas card) but one heck of a lot of fun to drive, as I will explain later. James Z. and I became good friends and he would take me to monthly SREA (Society of Real Estate Appraisers) meetings and introduce me to his appraiser friends and associates. We would come into the office every morning, finish up the previous days work, make our appointments, and then dart out into the world for our field work. We would end the week at the local car wash before making our respective inspections before the weekend. I could normally look at a handful of properties on a typical Friday and be on the beach by 1:00 p.m. Life was good.

In those days, all of our reports were hand-written in ink. We would attach a Polaroid picture of each subject property to every appraisal. There was no regulation or licensing at this time. We had a sense of integrity and the thought of inflating a value never really entered our minds. James Z. would finish up his work by mid-afternoon and be able to perform some out-side appraisal work with a local Savings and Loan client he had. There always seemed to be work for a good, conscientious, and ethical appraiser.

Appraising wasn't without its moments. Imagine going through people's homes at dusk in areas like Compton and South Los Angeles. I name these two locations for this is where I have my most vivid memories. One day I was assigned an appraisal to perform in South Los Angeles, in May, 1974. This particular appraisal was on a vacant house that had been foreclosed on and my assignment was to value the property for sale by the lender. As I measured the house from the exterior, I heard the sound of a low-hovering helicopter. A police helicopter in Los Angeles is not unusual, but it was so low that it attracted my attention. As I continued to measure the house, I heard the screeching of tires coming down the street. All of a sudden, police cars were everywhere and policemen began exiting their cars with their guns drawn and aimed at me! I dropped my measuring stick and clipboard and my hands went up over my head in a matter of milliseconds. There must have been over fifteen cops, all of whom had me in their sights. They asked me what I was doing at this abandoned home and I explained to them that I was an appraiser performing an appraisal. They discussed the fact that the SLA (Symbionese Liberation Army) had robbed a sporting good store in nearby Inglewood that morning and that they were on the loose when they got the call that a man was trying to break into a vacant house. From the helicopter, it probably appeared to be a man with a rifle, as I rolled the measuring device over the exterior of the building from window to window. After showing the police business cards with my name and occupation printed on them, they let me go.

I finished my inspection and headed home, where I watched the entire SLA shoot-out on television, just blocks from where I had been earlier that day. Talk about timing! I later did an appraisal on a house located one to two blocks from the burned-down SLA house in South Los Angeles. As I measured the house, I came across bullets embedded in the siding of the home. I later found out that more ammunition was fired into the SLA hideout than was fired in the entire Watts Riots of 1965, which lasted for six days, years before! The neighborhood was littered with bullets.

As I mentioned before, driving the Ford Torino was loads of fun. The main reason was that there was a popular television show on at the time called *Police Story*, created by novelist, and former Los Angeles police officer, Joseph Wambaugh. Every detective on the show drove a fleet-style Ford Torino, just like my company car. On many occasions I would be sitting in my Torino in South Los Angeles with the window down, dressed in my collared shirt (complete with tie and slacks), writing up an appraisal. As neighbors and punks would walk down the street, they would circle the car and yell epithets like "Pig!" That will get your heart racing. Most of the time I would just start up the car and move it to a location around the corner.

Going through other people's homes can be a really personal experience. I once entered a bathroom to find a shrine dedicated to Vladimir Lenin, complete with pictures and offerings. On another occasion, I performed an appraisal for a former member of the Black Panther Party. On still another occasion, I appraised a house for a former member of the Nazi Army in Europe during World War II. Have you ever met a Nazi?

Making an inspection of someone's abode really gives you insight into a person's life. I once noticed a gold, forty-five rpm record mounted in a frame along the hallway of a home. When I inquired about it, the woman stated that her ex-husband was Dr. Hook and he was awarded the record for selling a million copies. I asked her why she had it, not him. She turned to me and said, "I won it in the divorce settlement!"

I remember appraising a very large mansion in the Saratoga, California foothills. Once entering the home, I was astonished to find crayon marks and lines on almost every wall in the house. Another home I appraised was in Perris, California many years ago. It was a small ranchette located in Riverside County on a few acres in a rural setting. The mortgage company I worked for had foreclosed and it was supposed to be vacant. Upon my arrival, the first thing I noticed was that the kitchen cabinets and appliances were resting in the front yard. I soon entered the home, which was easy because there was no front door, and found chickens and horses taking up residence in the home. In the rear yard were other kinds of farm animals including cows, pigs, sheep, and even llamas. I had never seen so many animals with the run of a house before. I have never been foreclosed on before, but I imagine what a desperate time that must be for a borrower, especially this one. A person that leaves their animals behind must really be desperate.

This one situation aside, I have always enjoyed going through borrowers homes. It was like a window into their personal lives—very revealing.

My Introduction to "Persuasion"

During the mid 1970s, I drew weary of appraising and of my life in general. I was still in the Los Angeles area (Arcadia to be exact) and was tired of commuting on slow-moving freeways, breathing the smog-filled air, and going to the overcrowded beaches. All of a sudden, I met a girl with whom I became quite smitten and we decided to get married. While I was traveling for the Colwell Company once a month in Northern California, I met the wife of a contractor client who was getting into real estate in San Jose, California. She was an over-the-top type of personality and she convinced me I would do well in real estate sales. Really? Me?

So I quit my job with The Colwell Company, got married, moved to Northern California, and jumped into the real estate business, all within a two month period. Well,

I wasn't the worst real estate agent you ever met, but I was close. I hated it! I hated the less-than-honorable tactics used by brokers and I hated the way real estate agents stab each other in the back. Everything is commission first and the "Art of the Deal." If you don't understand that aspect of it, stay away!

After a couple of years of languishing in sales, I returned to appraising. I stumbled across a company run by two partners and soon started working for them. This company had six to ten appraisers at any given time and the company was doing appraisals all over the San Francisco Bay Area for many finance companies including Household Finance, Dial Finance, Avco Finance, Beneficial Finance, and others. I once again became enthusiastic with the appraisal process.

Over time, the partners split up and I was moved up to Vice President of Operations. In those days, there was no such thing as appraiser licenses. An affiliation with, or better yet, a designation with, a national organization such as the Society of Real Estate Appraisers or MAI (Member of the Appraisal Institute) would help one's credibility in the industry. However, anyone could appraise anything as long as the client thought the appraiser and appraisal report was credible. As a matter of fact, let's just stick with "anyone could appraise anything." That would come back to haunt the industry in the 1980s with the Savings and Loan debacle. I, myself, appraised a golf course, restaurants, motels ... you name it. I'm not saying I am, or was, incompetent; I am just making the point that anybody could appraise anything, generally without any oversight.

Around 1979, after becoming vice president of the firm, I had a request to do an appraisal for a Dr. Dewayne

Christensen, a dentist-turned-savings-and-loan-executive in Southern California. He requested I do an appraisal on a large vacant parcel of land in South San Jose that was zoned for condominiums that his North America Savings had purchased for development. He instructed me to do whatever research I needed to do, but I only had to give him a "letter appraisal," stating the value of the subject property was "no less" than my opinion of value.

This was not going to be a difficult assignment because I was already performing appraisals in a similar project only one block away and was very familiar with the neighborhood. I also had intimate knowledge of another land sale that was less than one mile from the subject property, having been a close friend to the sellers' son.

After completing the assignment, I mailed the letter with my opinion of value to Dr. Christensen and was quickly criticized for incompetence and general lack of knowledge of the area. This was, of course, typical for the independent-fee appraiser and still is today. I was yelled at, cussed at, threatened, and bullied. I stood my ground, as I knew this market, location, and what the units would finally sell for. Not surprisingly, Dr. Christensen put a "stop-payment" on the check soon after receiving the letter appraisal. I had many discussions with the owner of the appraisal company I worked for and he seemed to agree with me. Soon after the discussions, I left the firm due to unrelated circumstances.

I later learned that the owner of the company had revised the value of the appraisal (upward) and the stop-payment was removed from the check. I returned to the appraisal firm after a time but my checks started to bounce or not be issued at all. I continued to perform appraisals for the firm, but without receiving income, I reluctantly decided to open my own company. I figured that it would be less work to not do the appraisal and not get paid than to do the work and not get paid. Too bad I outgrew my fondness for lying on the beach.

After incorporating my company in 1982 and suffering through a slow start, I began to pick up a number of clients, mostly mortgage companies. One company in particular started giving me most of my business. I had a bad feeling about this because it put me in a very vulnerable position. What if the company decided to take its business elsewhere? I slowly began to expand beyond this one particular client and that turned out to be a good decision. I was soon contacted by three managers of the mortgage company about meeting for cocktails after work. The four of us discussed our relationship and the relationship that these three managers had experienced with appraisers in the past.

They all indicated that they were satisfied with my work and the appraisals were good, but that prior relationships with other appraisers had always proved to be a little more fruitful. I started to get really nervous at their implication, but I listened. They asked if I liked doing appraisals for their firm and I let them know I did. They stated that they were prepared to increase the volume of business and that they wanted me to increase my fees for the work. My first reaction was excitement, but that was short-lived. They proceeded to tell me that they had never done business with an appraiser that didn't kick something back to them and they expected me to do the same. My excitement turned to horror in less than ten seconds. I thought about it for thirty seconds and asked if I would

still get business from them if I didn't give them kickbacks. The answer was plain enough ... "No."

They told me that they expected the difference between
my normal fees and the increase in the new appraisal fees
was to be paid back to them at the end of each month.
They even gave me a code name to write the checks out
to. With few prospects at that given moment, I reluctantly
agreed. I went home feeling sick to my stomach. I was a
lost soul. I will never forget this moment as long as I live.
This isn't what my dad taught me. This was not "Keeping
my nose clean," as Dick H. had schooled me. I felt what
a lot of appraisers feel at one time or another ... the need
to survive.

Then, as if a miracle had happened, the mortgage company took longer and longer to pay, up to three months.
When asked by the "Big Three" about their secret checks,
I simply stated the truth. "I had not been paid." This went
on for some time and I never paid those bastards one red
cent! I had conned the cons! I remember one of the three
saying to me at one point, "You don't have any larceny in
you, do you?" By the time they left the mortgage company
a few months later, I had many more clients and never
dealt with those three again.

I developed a better relationship with the owners of the
mortgage company than with the "Big Three" managers
over the next few years. In fact, one owner always seemed
to display great excitement when I would show up in his
office and he always treated me well. He thought I was a
good appraiser and he wasn't afraid to tell people so when
asked for a name of a reputable appraiser. This resulted in
many appraisal assignments from him and others.

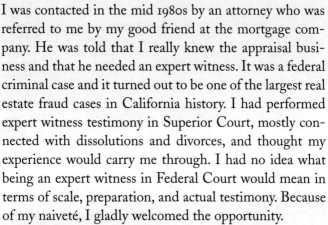

I was contacted in the mid 1980s by an attorney who was referred to me by my good friend at the mortgage company. He was told that I really knew the appraisal business and that he needed an expert witness. It was a federal criminal case and it turned out to be one of the largest real estate fraud cases in California history. I had performed expert witness testimony in Superior Court, mostly connected with dissolutions and divorces, and thought my experience would carry me through. I had no idea what being an expert witness in Federal Court would mean in terms of scale, preparation, and actual testimony. Because of my naiveté, I gladly welcomed the opportunity.

The case was United States vs. George I. Benny, a real estate developer from Hillsborough, California. He had purchased a large apartment building, known as Diamond Heights Village, in San Francisco, consisting of hundreds of units overlooking San Francisco and Daly City. Using the services of complicit real estate agents and title officers, Benny was able to perpetrate the ultimate "No Money Down" scheme.

The bank loaning the money for the purchase, Wells Fargo, was duped into thinking Benny was paying $14.5 million for the property when, in fact, he was only paying $12.5 million. According to court documents (Unites States of America, Plaintiff, Appellee v. George I. Benny, Defendant, Appellant-United States Court of Appeals for the Ninth Circuit), Benny represented to Wells Fargo that he had put $2 million of his own money into the purchase. The $2 million check was written on an account with a balance of only $5,000. Neither Benny nor the escrow company notified Wells Fargo when the check was dishonored. On the basis of Benny's representations, Wells Fargo loaned Benny $13.5 million to buy Diamond Heights in November of 1977. One does have to wonder, however, who performed the appraisal on the project that Wells Fargo based their loan on. Was it a staff appraiser for Wells Fargo or did the bank base their loan on an appraiser hired by Benny?

This loan deceit regarding the purchase was not the only thing Benny had up his sleeve. He began to convert the apartments into condominiums at the end of a real estate cycle and that translated into slow sales. In fact, the sales became so slow that Benny began to bring in "straw buyers" in order to stimulate sales and defraud lenders into making loans based on bogus transactions.

The defendants inflated the purchase price of the Diamond Heights units in order to obtain loans larger than what otherwise would have been available. Since the "straw sales" did not involve actual arm's length negotiations, Benny himself set the sales prices at levels that far exceeded the actual market value of the units. Believing these sales to be the result of arm's length transactions, appraisers for the lenders and the mortgage brokers relied upon them to determine the value of the units on which new loans were being sought; these resulted in inflated appraisals. Consequently, banks and mortgage brokers made loans on the units in excess of their actual market value (Unites States of America, Plaintiff, Appellee v. George I. Benny, Defendant, Appellant-United States Court of Appeals for the Ninth Circuit April 15, 1986).

When he ran out of his own straw buyers, he started to make them up, using the information left on sales cards from the condo sales office. I was told that the straw buyers didn't even know their names and information were being used. One of the unwitting buyers was an assistant district attorney for the County of San Francisco. When his loan application ended up on the desk of a CalFed (California Federal Savings) executive who knew him, he was contacted by the executive via a phone call. The executive said he didn't know he was buying a condominium in Diamond Heights and the lawyer replied that he wasn't. This, as it was reported to me, started the whole criminal investigation.

This case involved some of the biggest names at the time in the lending industry: Wells Fargo Bank, Crocker Bank, Security Pacific National Bank, Imperial Savings, CalFed, American Savings, Home Savings, and many more.

After qualifying as an "expert witness," I was on the stand for a full four days. I gave depositions in front of FBI agents, was served a subpoena to appear in court, not by a process server, but a postal inspector, and spent every waking moment preparing for the case. The judge in the case was Robert F. Peckham, also known in some circles as the "Hanging Judge." He later had the Federal Building in San Jose, California named after him.

After being found guilty of twenty-one counts of mail fraud and one count of racketeering, Benny was sentenced by Judge Peckham to thirty years in federal custody, serving part of his term at Leavenworth, KS. At the time, the San Francisco Examiner wrote extensively on the subject as the Benny case progressed. The Diamond Heights property was not the only property Benny was connected to. He was also connected to a 2300-acre ranch near Reno, Nevada called the Double Diamond Ranch(on which he intended to build a planned community), a 160-unit condominium complex in Las Vegas known as the Casablanca Condominium Project, the former San Francisco Armory, and the infamous "Carolands" mansion in Hillsborough, California.

I remember one weekend night during the trial, I was at Benny's residence (also in Hillsborough) discussing the case and my testimony when I was asked to stay for dinner with Benny and the lawyers. "I have to get home to my wife and need to leave," I explained. "Nonsense," said Benny. "I will send my car and driver to pick her up." And he did. My wife was picked up some forty-five minutes later in a Rolls Royce and chauffeured back to Benny's mansion. I was in my early thirties but was still impressionable. Benny took us down to his wine cellar that was situated in the side of a small hill below his residence. The giant iron doors were unlocked, thrown open and inside were stacks and stacks of vintage champagne piled from floor to ceiling. He introduced me to fine French champagne after clutching four or five bottles of Louis Roeder, Dom Runart, and, of course, Dom Perignon, and we then returned to his house for an evening of culture with several members of the San Francisco Ballet.

Benny owned the "Carolands" mansion for a short time. It was a magnificent French Chateau consisting of 68,000 square feet with ninety-eight rooms that had fallen into a state of disrepair and neglect. I think Benny only lived in it a short time. I really don't know if he sold it or it was confiscated by the government or bankruptcy court. Rumor had it that John F. Kennedy had spent the night there years ago and even considered it for a western White House. But it became even more renowned as the site for another infamous crime: the beating and raping (and eventual death of one) of two high school students brutalized by a security guard hired to protect the property. The property was eventually acquired and brought back to its former splendor. I was fortunate to tour the mansion as it was one of the "showcase" homes used to benefit local charities in the area. Each room had been assigned to a different interior designer and it was simply glorious!

I feel I had been lucky to have been connected to a part of real estate history in Northern California. I once attended a seminar and dinner in Emoryville, California, where an FBI agent was addressing the audience and discussing real estate fraud. He talked a lot about the Benny case, as did most of the agents in his San Francisco field office. They were proud of their involvement and their help with the conviction.

Appraising Takes True Grit

As we progressed into the 1980s, the lending industry, under the leadership of Ronald Reagan, became more and more "de-regulated." I would like to make a point here. I have never seen de-regulation work in any industry. I say this knowing full well that I will get more than a few criticisms on this, but I have never seen it work—not in the airline industry, not in the phone industry, not in the energy industry (think Enron), and certainly not in lending and investment banking on Wall Street. It just doesn't work. At the expense of using an overworked cliché, it's like giving the fox the keys to the chicken coop.

I don't think President Reagan understood this. He was for less government and that was that. What he failed to understand was that by de-regulating, you hand the keys over to the fox.

Builders, real estate brokers and executives, and anybody and everybody that had a connection to real estate was buying or starting savings & loans after de-regulation. Prior to this de-regulation, S & L's pretty much had to stick with lending on residential properties. How boring. Commercial banks made loans to developers and commercial/industrial investors, not Savings & Loans. Well, that all changed. Your local S & L could now loan on commercial ventures, exotic properties, windmills, you name it and anyone could appraise them!

What was also happening at this time was the proliferation of mortgage brokers in the lending community. There had always been brokers, but during this period they were growing at a rapid rate. These brokers put additional pressure on the appraisal industry in the form of pushing values. Most S & Ls held onto a certain amount of the loans they originated, with the rest being sold off into the secondary markets (FNMA and Freddie Mac). But the mortgage brokers held no mortgages on their books. It's a different mind-set when it's not your money or the money of your depositors, as we would see in 2007.

In my business, we were overwhelmed with business from mortgage brokers. This came as interest rates hovered around 10 percent. Every time rates got close to 10 percent, we would get busy. It was a threshold for many years. In fact, I remember 10 percent being a reasonable rate in 1974 and it continued to be, up until Federal Reserve Chairman Alan Greenspan began his loosening of credit in the 1990s.

During the early 1980s, I felt another need to diversify, so I explored the possibility of doing appraisals for FHA and the HUD program. There was quite a turnout at the HUD offices in San Francisco consisting of numerous appraisers that had the same idea as I. There must have been sixty appraisers that wanted to be on the FHA appraisal panel. The way it worked was that there was a list of appraisers that FHA approved to be on their roster. They would be on a rotating basis and no lender would be able to select the appraiser that would be performing the assignment. Novel idea, wasn't it?

What would soon happen, however, was that under the "Direct Endorsement" program, participating lenders would be able to have their own appraiser or staff appraiser perform the appraisal in order to streamline the process. Here we come back to that "fox and the chicken coop" again. This gave the lender complete control over the appraiser and the process.

The appraisals themselves involved a lot of superfluous components, such as giving borrowers ways to increase their energy efficiency. Isn't that a job for the utility company? We also had to perform the appraisals cheaply. They were substantially under the market price for an appraisal. I guess that is why so many appraisers dropped out of the program. I know that when I can get more money for my services, I would normally look elsewhere, and I did.

Fannie Mae (Federal National Mortgage Association) also had an approved appraiser list prior to the early 1980s. I still remember my approved appraiser number: #1182829. At this time, each appraiser had to get approved by FNMA in order to perform appraisals for lenders that sold loans to Fannie. An appraiser could not get approved with them directly. You had to have a correspondent lender sponsor you. The Colwell Company was my sponsor.

At some point, they changed the way this was done. Suddenly, it was up to the lender to maintain an approved appraiser list and carefully review their work. If something should go wrong, like a fraudulent appraisal, the lender was obligated to buy the loan back from FNMA under a "Repurchase Agreement." That tends to keep the lender honest because too many repurchases can get expensive. That same repurchase agreement doesn't work so well with mortgage brokers or mortgage bankers who aren't well capitalized, as we would find out in the new millennium.

In the mid 1980s, I again grew tired of dealing with mortgage brokers. I made a contact with FNMA and decided that if anyone wanted an honest appraisal, it was Fannie Mae. I started performing appraisals for their foreclosure department. I also made several contacts in the mortgage insurance industry and started doing appraisals for MGIC and others. They wanted honest appraisals because they were insuring 90 and 95 percent loans.

I was also doing a lot of builder business at this time. I had one client named Lantern Mortgage Company, which was owned by a man named Floyd S., in San Jose, California. Floyd was ambitious and so was I. He would spend weekends with several builders whom he had made friends with at their sales offices on newly constructed subdivisions. He would take the loan application right on the spot, the moment the builder had a prospect. Monday morning would roll around and he would have a pile of loan applications. I liked the way Floyd worked—hard!

Then it came to my attention that Floyd was brokering the loans through a primary lender or wholesale lender that was part of CitiFed, a national savings and loan out of New York State that is no longer in business. The branch manager was contacting each borrower of Floyd's and telling every one of them that he could do the loan slightly cheaper if they would switch and go through him. I won't mention the branch manager's name, but rumor has it that shortly thereafter he was fired, but then turned around, sued the bank for wrongful termination, and won!

I am told that one of the first things that they teach you in law school is that there is no right and wrong. I could never be an attorney. I see most everything as right or wrong.

The builder business became very profitable for me. They wanted a discount because of volume, but once you had the project set up, it almost became a matter of "cookie-cutters" because every house was so similar. I did a lot of builder business in the mid to late 1980s and was getting quite a lot of referrals. One day I received a call from a mortgage company in San Mateo County that claimed to have an exclusive arrangement with the developer of a condominium project in South San Jose to make all of the loans. They said they had eight units to start with and gave me the orders. I was doing quite a few projects in the area and knew the market well.

To my surprise, as I performed the research and analysis necessary to develop my conclusions, I realized that this was the same project that I performed a letter appraisal on for Dr. Christensen years before. Things do certainly come back around. After looking at the contracts, I realized that the sale prices were 30–40 percent over similar type units in the same market area. I quickly called the lender and told him that I could not justify the values they reported getting. He told me to cancel the appraisal orders. I did cancel the requests, but I followed the progress of the project with great interest. You see, I don't think much of crooks and I think they give all of us in the real estate business a bad name. There are now more crooks in the business than ever.

I found out who eventually performed the reports and got a hold of a copy of one of the appraisals. It was an appraisal company that had a lot of previous dealings with that branch manager at Citifed. To use another cliché: Birds of a feather always flock together! I examined the report and found that the appraiser had gone over five to eight miles for comparable sales. The one element that made this necessary to the appraiser was the fact that the project had man-made streams. I'll tell you what made it necessary to use comparable sales that far away: the high sales prices!

Eventually, I called the Federal Home Loan Bank Board in San Francisco. I had followed the county records on the project and found that if the sales price of one of the units was $105,000, the first mortgage was approximately $103,000. This was repeated over and over. Just like in the past few years, there was no "Skin in the Game," or equity. The lien-holder (or mortgagor) was none other than North America Savings in Anaheim, California. The same S & L owned and managed by Dr. Christensen. He was closing these loans with depositor's money! I thought the shareholders would like to know, too. I explained all of this to the employee at the Federal Home Loan Bank Board and he told me that they could do nothing until the "sh*t hit the fan." Boy, did it.

Finally, in 1987, the business was liquidated by the Federal Savings & Loan Insurance Corporation at a cost of $120 million. That was big bucks in 1987.

Funny thing, on the way to a meeting with federal regulators who were about to seize the institution, Dr. Christensen committed suicide by driving his Jaguar into a concrete bridge abutment on a freeway and was killed instantly. I guess you could say it finally hit the fan. I can't believe I have known so many big-time operators.

In 1986, the interest rates on first mortgages dropped below 10 percent, which, as I stated before, had been a threshold for many years. This started a stampede of refinancing. I had six appraisers working for my firm and at one point, had over three hundred appraisal requests that we couldn't even get to. I remember writing on the blackboard that was located in our workroom that, "History is being made." Borrowers and clients alike would call and inquire about the status of their appraisal. It was so busy that we spent most of our time looking up the status of any given request and falling more behind on the actual appraisals.

Offers of bribes were commonplace. Borrowers and clients offered to double, even triple, the fees if we would move the request to the top of the heap. It eventually got to the point where I called our local newspaper, *The San Jose*

Mercury News, and told a reporter of our dilemma. They jumped on the idea and then wrote a full page article on the "bottlenecking of the appraisal process." The morning the article ran, I was performing an appraisal on a duplex and the borrower asked me, "Aren't you the appraiser in the article?" I had become a celebrity. This took a couple of years to work through. Soon enough, things would get slow again.

About this time, another broker client took me to lunch at a fancy restaurant. He told me how good an appraiser I was and that he appreciated my hard work and ethics. Then he told me that he could no longer use my services as we were too conservative and he couldn't seem to put loans together with our "low-ball" values. Ouch.

This is the way it has always been. It takes a certain amount of grit to stand up to it. I have managed to do it for over thirty-five years but it is finally started to catch up with me.

A long-time client, a mortgage company, eventually pressed me on values and analysis after years of doing business together. It was a hard-money lender, meaning that they would procure investors for funds to loan and then find borrowers to lend to. Since most of the borrowers were what we today call "sub-prime," the realistic valuation of the collateral was paramount.

I liked doing appraisals for this firm, as they were realistic when it came to valuations and they never attempted to get me to raise the value. I must mention here that over the past thirty-five years, I have performed a substantial number of appraisals for hard-money lenders and most, at some point, start taking a more liberal look at property values and almost always insist on higher values. This is most typically tied to loan volume. As the volume goes down in a normal real estate related business cycle, the pressure for higher values goes up. The slower the demand for loans, the lower the quality of appraisals. This is why most of the hard-money lenders I have known over the years are no longer in business. The people I feel sorry for are the investors who put their trust and faith in these lenders and end up with notes and mortgages on "junk" properties that are not only over-valued, but less than prime properties, as well.

This particular client hired a young, aggressive loan officer who had happened to have taken a real estate appraisal course. What amazed me is that he often used what little knowledge he had acquired in class to argue for higher values. Never mind what prudent appraisal practice would dictate, he would find some exception to the rule and try to apply it to benefit his cause.

This finally led to a confrontation over a single family residence zoned for commercial use on an appraisal I had performed. A debate ensued over the "Highest and Best Use" of the property and I would not give in and stood my ground. They were brokering the loan to a wholesaler and did not care whether the appraisal was performed correctly. They knew they couldn't sell the loan if I wrote up the report as I had outlined to them during our discussions. This one transaction ended a relationship of over ten years.

I recently read a *Wall Street Journal* article about the saga of a blue house in Arizona and its owner's successful attempts to procure credit lines and the eventual refinance of the property through a mortgage broker. It was built on blocks and consisted of approximately 600 square feet.

This reminded me of several episodes over the years where I have found myself in the position of appraising "substandard" housing. The best advice I can give another appraiser, novice, or seasoned professional, is "walk away."

Back in the 1980s, I was approached by an accountant to inspect a piece of property that he had placed a private mortgage on. I knew the accountant, as he shared office space with one of my mortgage broker clients. What he was doing in addition to his tax practice was making hard-money loans on behalf of a group of his tax clients to borrowers that were probably finding it difficult to borrow through normal channels. This particular transaction resulted in a lawsuit against the accountant, as the loan he had made went into foreclosure, and he put me in contact with his attorney. My instructions were to estimate fair market value of the property that secured the loan.

I set up an appointment to meet the accountant at the property, which was located on the side of a hill in the Santa Cruz Mountains and was somewhat secluded. The property turned out to be nothing but a shack. There was no concrete foundation or footings, no electricity, and no running water, with the exception of a half-inch galvanized pipe running from a neighbor. Heck, there wasn't even a front door ... you had to climb up a ladder to access the shack from below and crawl through an opening in the floor. I remember commenting that this wasn't a house. He replied that it wasn't always in that condition. When he loaned on the structure, it was a house. Nice try. I returned to the office and immediately called the attorney. I said I wasn't interested in being involved in the case and that if I had been one of the investors, I would have sued, too! After explaining the situation as I saw it, the attorney thanked me for my time and insight. I told him that I was willing to chalk up any time I had invested to experience.

Lenders today all underwrite their loans to sell off to the secondary market (Fannie Mae and Freddie Mac), or to other investors and government entities like FHA. Very few lenders "warehouse" (keep in their own portfolio) loans anymore. In the 1970s, Pasadena Federal Savings in Pasadena, California was known for its "portfolio" loans and were extremely picky on what properties they would lend on. These properties had to be "prime" properties, meaning no busy streets, no fixer-uppers, no one-bed-room homes, and no white elephants. If they were going to get a property back, it was going to be a prime prop-erty with no marketability problems attached to it. This is one of the main reasons for the lack of confidence in the mortgage markets today. Just like the sub-prime bor-rower, most mortgage lender's of the past ten years have had very little "Skin in the game." Everybody(originating lender) is poised to stick the other guy(investor). A simple solution is to have mortgage lenders retain a percentage of their loans as portfolio loans. Maybe 30% of their total originations would have to be held. And not just 30% of their choosing. The 30% would be selected at random. This would cleanup underwriting in a hurry. Over the years, underwriting standards have become more relaxed (absurdly so) and not much concern has been made with regards to the property or its condition or any physical deficiencies. Some times it's just better to walk away and forget about being paid. Money isn't everything. What I learned from the Benny case is to perform every appraisal like you have to defend it on the stand. I am very careful about what appraisals I put my name on.

Another observation I have made over the years is that the more bedrooms, the better. Prospective buyers that are interested in three- and four-bedroom homes would not even look at or consider a two-bedroom home. A two-bedroom home has limited marketability because of this factor. If you are going to appraise a two-bedroom home, you *must* utilize at least a few two bedroom comparables. This is a market unto itself. When you appraise a one-bedroom home, the market is even more scarce. In fact, I can't remember performing an appraisal on a one-bedroom home unless there were plenty of one-bedroom comparables in the subject market area. This is seldom the case. This is especially true for small 600 square foot homes and smaller. The 600 square foot structure is not much larger than my two-car garage.

This is also my view when it comes to homes that lack foundations. No concrete foundation, no appraisal. On one occasion in the 1980s, I was to perform an appraisal on a small ranchette-type property in Gilroy, California, a small community about fifty miles south of San Jose. As I was measuring the structure, I noticed that the exterior stucco extended down the side of the house and seemed to "spill" out over the dirt. I poked around with a stick and learned that there was no foundation. *None.* I packed my things and drove off. I later called the mortgage broker client and informed them of my findings. He said not to worry and immediately called another appraiser. I was on pretty good terms with this broker and asked if I could see the others appraisers report when he received it.

Once I had received the copy and examined it, I wasn't too shocked to see the same name that had been on Dr. Christensen's appraisals that I had turned down in South San Jose. The first thing I looked at was the foundation description and found the little box for "concrete foundation" checked. I'm sure glad my name wasn't on the bottom of that report.

The primary scope of the appraisal is the property and its surroundings. It is not our job to assess the risk or credit-worthiness of the borrower. That doesn't stop some mortgage brokers from trying, however. I remember a case where I was asked to appraise a property in the "Rose Garden" area of San Jose, California. Upon my inspection, I quickly learned that the owners were not only living in the property, but were also using it as some kind of aviary. I mean there were hundreds, if not thousands, of birds flying everywhere: the living room, kitchen, bedroom, and baths … everywhere. There was also feces and birdseed everywhere. It all showed up in my pictures and I had described my observations in great detail. That is where the rub came in.

I was asked by the mortgage broker to give him a few minutes to go over the appraisal, which I gladly did. His main focus was trying to get me to eliminate all reference to the birds. He explained that the borrower was otherwise credit-worthy, paid his bills on time, had an excellent job history, and was deserving of this loan that the broker was about to make him. Why should I want to penalize him because of his hobby? I replied to him that I was not penalizing him. I was simply performing my job in describing the property. Part of that assessment was current condition of the property. If I was to compare this property to recent sales in the neighborhood, I would have to adjust the sales to reflect the overall condition of the subject property. In making this adjustment, I would have to explain why I felt that the subject property was inferior to similar homes in the neighborhood. This is where the birds came in. I also owe it to the client (who is *not* the borrower) and subsequent clients (that may change depending on how often the loan is sold) who depend on my analysis, observations, and conclusions in order to determine the risk associated with this loan for it is they, not me, that assesses that risk.

Performing the Appraisal

Appraising is not rocket science. It often takes a little detective work, a lot of common sense, and the ability to stand up to a lot of critics, because you *will* have them, no matter what. To its credit, the industry has evolved over the past thirty years in furthering the education of each one of its participants through licensing and continuing educational requirements. As new laws and regulations are put in place, the industry does a pretty good job of keeping its members informed. This educational process is only a small component of the job description, however. The main quality of a good appraiser is not so much knowledge, but integrity. An appraiser must have integrity above all, for if it is not present, all the knowledge in the world will not compensate for it.

This requirement of integrity is not stressed enough, in my humble opinion, yet it is the foundation of the industry. I don't know how you test for it or if it is something that can be taught. Maybe it comes from one's upbringing or maybe you are born with it. The words "ethics" and "integrity" are thrown around quite a bit in the real estate and lending industries, but I honestly don't see much of it in practice. It's as basic as knowing right from wrong. Yet, over the past thirty-five years, I have reviewed hundreds of appraisals where the appraiser did not seem to know right from wrong and did not even seem to care about such things. Maybe my world is too black and white. It bothers me when somebody runs a red light, parks in a handicapped space without a handicapped sticker visible, cuts in a line, is tardy, or talks down to a person that they feel is beneath them.

Let's assume you have the integrity. How, then, do you go about appraising a property? I will try to give a brief, overall, and perhaps even an over-simplified description of the process here. There are many books and publications that cover the actual art of appraising in the marketplace.

The first step in the process is to inspect the subject property and see what exactly we are valuing. This might seem obvious at first but over the years, the appraisal process has changed to the extent that even this first step has been, on many occasions, eliminated. With the introduction of the FNMA form #2055, the interior inspection and rear view of the subject property has been eliminated. What this amounts to is essentially a "drive-by" appraisal, meaning we appraisers don't even get out of our car. Following close behind the drive-by appraisal is the AVM, or "automated valuation model," where no inspection is made at all.

The inspection will normally start with measuring the structure in order to determine the actual size or square footage of the building. As we will compare the subject to other similar properties, we want to locate sales that closely resemble the subject with respect to overall livable area and the overall size of the site or lot size. The likelihood that we will find three to five sales exactly like the subject property is pretty remote unless it is a subdivision or tract of similar homes (typically newer homes). More established neighborhoods normally consist of homes of various ages, styles, and sizes. In the case of the more established neighborhoods, it is advisable to "bracket sales," meaning to analyze both larger and smaller homes, as well as those similar in size to the subject.

Part of the inspection process is to evaluate the floor plan or flow of traffic through the house. This is not as difficult as it might seem. Most deficiencies or cases of "functional obsolescence" stand out, for example, the presence of a "tandem" bedroom arrangement. This is where one must go through one bedroom in order to access another bedroom. This is more common than you think. I believe that most of these situations were created by room additions where the owner just stuck a room addition on the back of an existing home with no regard to traffic flow.

Another example is found in my neighbor's home. Upon entering the home, you are immediately in the dining room. What were they thinking? Although seeing the problem is often easy, finding solutions is often difficult, but necessary in the valuation process. If the deficiency is easily corrected, the value of the property might not suffer much. However, if the obsolescence is not easily corrected or the cost to cure is significant, the value of the subject property could suffer greatly. If the obsolescence is "incurable," more discussion and analysis is warranted.

The interior inspection will also disclose deferred maintenance issues, such as dry rot and water damage, most often found in bathroom inspections. Although the appraiser is not typically licensed or qualified to properly assess these types of damage, the appraiser can normally call for an expert's opinion of the situation and make his/ her opinion of value subject to the outcome of any such professional, outside inspections. These are not limited to, but may include, termite inspections, roof inspections, construction inspections, foundation reports, and any other inspections by qualified experts in fields that might impact the value of the property.

When so much information about the subject property is gathered by the physical inspection of the interior and this information can have such a major impact on the ultimate valuation of the property, it is more than curious to me why an underwriter or lender would call for a "drive-by" appraisal report.

I assume that the original idea behind the #2055 report was to save the borrower money if the value was not considered to be an issue with respect to underwriting the loan, i.e. a low LTV (loan to value ratio). These #2055s became very popular when writing home equity loans, HELOCs, and second trust deeds. Appraisers charged less for them as they didn't have to take the time to set and schedule appointments to see the interiors of the properties and the reports themselves were brief and took little time to fill out.

However, at some point, the form was redesigned and actually took as much time to complete as a full appraisal known as the form #1004. In typical fashion, the fee appraisers received for these #2055s did not increase with the added workload. Various versions of these forms have come and gone, with new versions being introduced often, but their use remains popular.

After making the initial inspection, it is common practice for the appraiser to start the comparable sale selection. The best place to start this process is with sales that are in the same or similar market area as subject and have the greatest degrees of similarity to the subject property such as livable area, site influences, and amenities. It is also important to utilize sales that have sold as recently as possible to reflect any run-up of values in the area or any downward trends. When sales are difficult to come by, the appraiser must expand his search criteria and geographical boundaries, making sure that he/she is not utilizing market data that would then result in an inflated appraisal or an appraisal that would be too low.

For example, over the years I have seen situations where one home that is almost identical to another on the same street sell for substantially more than the other because of different mailing addresses (one city or town having more "snob appeal" than the other), or by school district boundaries where one school district has a higher rating than another. The appraiser must be able to make these distinctions about the neighborhoods and be aware of factors that are not easily evident from just making an inspection of the property. I have reviewed reports where the appraiser might have traveled hundreds of miles to perform the appraisal. This, in most cases, is probably not a good idea and makes a strong case for using a local appraiser that is familiar with these aspects of the local market.

In many cases, appraisers that perform appraisals outside a reasonable geographical radius lack the essential tools to complete the job such as data sources. These data sources could include, but are not limited to, a local MLS, or "Multiple Listing Service." This is a crucial tool, as most properties that have sold are listed on this service and most MLSs list details about each sale that could not possibly be found using county records or other databases. Factors that could affect the sales price might include any remodeling that has been performed and sales concessions that the seller may have helped the buyer with in order to facilitate the sale, etc. It could quite possibly detail any factors that might affect value, like physical deficiencies such as foundation problems, or the home at one time being a major crime scene that attracted regional or national headlines. All these factors could have an impact on value.

After all of the data that is considered pertinent to the analysis of the subject property is collected, it is time to verify the data. Sometimes this can be an easy process, but most of the time it is the most time-consuming, least satisfying part of the job. This might include calling the real estate agent involved with a particular sale and procuring details about the sale from this person. Asking the agent to elaborate on the condition of the property or maybe the status of permits on a room addition are all common questions that might not be found elsewhere. It is also a good idea (and most of the time a requirement) to verify all data with a disinterested third-party, such as the county records or a title company, for accuracy of the MLS data, e.g. sales prices, dates of sale, and any other information those records might report.

Once the sales data has been acquired and verified, it is time to perform the actual analysis. When making a comparison, the appraiser studies each comparable sale and compares it to the subject, making adjustments for each component that is considered superior, inferior, or similar to the subject property. For example, if sale #1 sold for $200,000 and had a swimming pool (and the subject did not), an adjustment might be made to the sale for $15,000 to reflect that the sale is superior to the subject, at least in this one respect. If all else is similar to subject, this $15,000 would be subtracted from the sales price of the comparable sale and give us an indicated value of $185,000.

This analysis is applied to each sale used for a basis of comparison and should, in the end, result in a narrow range of indicators for the subject property. Each indicated value is then examined and a determination is made about where to place the most emphasis. There is no averaging in this process. A few of the sales might receive more emphasis due to the timing of their sales, or maybe three of five sales might be closer in size to the subject property and thus will receive more emphasis. It is up to the good judgment and skill of the appraiser to determine this weighing of facts.

Just how does one know how much to attribute to a particular component? The short answer is to extract it from the market. This is often difficult, but it can be done. For instance, let's look at the swimming pool. In the above example, we used $15,000, but where did this figure come from? It hopefully came from a "paired-sale analysis." This simply means to find two recent sales in subject market area that are as close to each other in most respects (size of improvements, size of the site or lot, style, overall condition, amenities, etc.) but one has a pool and the other does not. After making adjustments for any elements that are dissimilar, the difference between the two is then attributed to the swimming pool. This method can be used to determine what the market will pay for bedrooms, guest houses, locations on busy streets, and other negative site influences. It is also used to determine how much to attribute to the passing of time, either when property values are going up or when they are going down. It is also a very convincing way to justify your adjustments when appearing on the stand in a courtroom. It simply comes across as more credible when you have a method for proving your opinions.

Careful attention should be paid to analyzing sales that share common attributes or deficiencies with the subject property, such as a location on a busy street. I have observed over the years several things when it comes to the influence of a busy street on the value of a property. First, there is normally no shortage of similar sales on a busy street. One would think that these properties would not change hands often because of the obvious detrimental nature of the busy artery, but that is not the case. These type of properties change hands often. I rarely have a difficult time locating sales on a busy street.

Second, it is not only the effects of fast-traveling cars, the noise, and imminent danger for pets and children, but also the accessibility problems associated with these type properties commonly referred to as "ingress" and "egress." It is often a nightmare to try to backup into traffic in order to exit the driveway on these properties.

After the sales data is analyzed and adjustments made, it is time to come up with a number or estimate the market value of the subject. Before we do, let's explore a little bit on what exactly market value is. Market value has been defined in several ways in the past: "(1) The highest price in terms of money that a property would bring in a competitive and open market under all conditions requisite to a fair sale, the buyer and seller each acting prudently and knowledgeably and assuming the price is not affected by undue stimulus. (2) The price at which a willing seller would sell and a willing buyer would buy, neither being under abnormal pressure. (3) The price expectable if a reasonable time is allowed to find a purchaser and if both seller and prospective buyer are fully informed." (The Appraisal of Real Estate-American Institute of Real Estate Appraisers of the National Association of Realtors 1978). Notice that it is stated as "The highest price."

Contrast that with today's definition of market value: "The most probable price which a property should bring in a competitive and open market under all conditions requisite to a fair sale, the buyer and seller, each acting prudently, knowledgeably and assuming the price is not affected by undue stimulus. Implicit in this definition is the consummation of a sale as of a specified date and the passing of title from seller to buyer under conditions whereby: (1) Buyer and seller are typically motivated. (2) Both parties are well-informed or well-advised, each acting in what he or she considers his or her own best interest. (3) A reasonable time is allowed for exposure in the open market. (4) Payment is made in terms of cash in U.S. Dollars or in terms of financial arrangements comparable thereto, and (5) the price represents the normal consideration for the property sold unaffected by special or creative financing or sales concessions granted by anyone associated with the sale." (Fannie Mae Form 1004 March 2005 - Freddie Mac Form 70 March 2005).

Probable price certainly makes more sense than highest price. Things don't always change for the worse but on occasion, things change for the better. However, judging by the conduct of most real estate agents, mortgage brokers, lenders, and borrowers, it's as if the old definition still stands. Again, to these players, highest is better.

Now that we have selected the sales, verified our data, and made adjustments to the comparables for the various differences, we must look at the indicators and estimate the value. As I stated before, we never average the sales or indicators. We look for the most similar sale to subject and the most recent sales for our emphasis. Hopefully, the spread between the indicators is not too great.

There are three approaches to value: the market approach (which we just discussed): the income approach, which analyzes the potential income stream of the property and by utilizing various indicators (such as gross rent multipliers) arrives at a value; and the cost approach, which basically analyzes the replacement cost or cost of the subject new, minus any physical, functional, or external depreciation, plus the value of any site improvements and the value of the land.

I won't go into all of these approaches in this book. The market approach is considered to be the best approach to value, as it most accurately gauges what the market is doing at any given time. There is much more to appraising than this brief overview, but I believe that this will make the process a little easier to understand for the uninitiated.

Mortgage Fraud

Volumes could be written about real estate and mortgage fraud, so I will keep the scope of my discussion of fraud narrow and only discuss fraud from a standpoint of how it relates to the appraisal process. You will find that in most cases of mortgage fraud, an appraiser is complicit in the act, but not always a knowing or willing participant.

This book originally started out as a documentary about the appraisal industry. I had lined up interviews with numerous appraisers, shot many of the interviews, and even performed a rough edit of them. I had, by coincidence, landed in the middle of the California Association of Mortgage Broker's annual convention in Long Beach, California in August 2007, as a result of accompanying my wife for a series of workshops that she was conducting at Long Beach State University at the time. Her hotel was the same hotel the Association was using for their convention. Lucky for me, I brought my camera, microphones, and related equipment and was capable of conducting interviews in my room.

I went down to a ballroom early the first morning and sat down at a table, alone. Numerous people came up to me and suggested I join them. I explained that I would prefer to just listen to the various speakers. I told them I was a filmmaker and was making a documentary about appraisers. Most were very cordial and even expressed an interest in being interviewed. Word must have gotten around as an official with the Association approached me and told me that I should speak with their media representative. I said I would and, after a few minutes, he came over and introduced himself. He sat down, asked me about my project, and said he could line up certain members to be interviewed. We exchanged cell phone numbers and I was told he would get back to me within thirty minutes.

After the thirty minutes went by, my cell phone rang. It was the media representative with some troubling, but not unexpected, news. He told the board of directors of my project and they quickly instructed me to stop all interviews with their members. No interviews would be allowed and it was their preference that I leave the premises. That was the end of my coverage of this very timely convention. I say this because the news had just broken about problems with Countrywide, the country's largest mortgage company. In fact, there was a network television news truck in front of the hotel. I walked over to it and asked the technician how their interviews were going with the group. He told me that they were not going well and that they could get little insight about the credit and sub-prime crisis from the members. He also said that he expected Countrywide to be bankrupt by the end of the week. He was a little off on the timing, but he was right with respect to the outcome. Countrywide was taken over by Bank of America.

After my wife's workshops, we drove over to Palm Springs for a few days in the hot sun. As my luck would have it, I was soon swimming in the pool with a gentleman who introduced himself as a mortgage broker from Los Angeles. I began to tell him of my documentary project and as time went on, I expressed an interest in interviewing him on-camera about the mortgage industry. He asked, "What specific topic would you like to ask me questions about?" I thought for a minute and replied that I would like to ask him questions about mortgage fraud.

"Fraud?" he fired back. "There hasn't been any fraud in the industry since the days of FHA!"

I was startled by his reply. "No fraud?" I fired back.

"Nope, no fraud" he replied.

This man was extremely naive, narrow-mined, or just plain trying to pull the wool over my eyes. I couldn't believe it. He told me that he would not consent to an interview and immediately got out of the pool. There I was, pondering just how widespread fraud was, and nobody was interested in exposing it, preventing it, or even talking about it. I had contacted numerous mortgage brokers and only one had committed to an interview. When the time came to shoot it, he was nowhere to be found. This was the final straw. There would be no documentary. All I had was interviews with appraisers and it appeared that the documentary would come across as a number of appraisers just complaining and whining.

I decided that with over thirty-five years in the business, I could tell the story as well as anyone, especially with all of the experiences that I could share with you, the reader. That is when I decided to write this book instead of producing a documentary.

I've always found the subject of fraud so curious. How does one prove fraud with respect to the appraisal? After all, the appraisal is just an opinion of value. There are few absolutes when it comes to analysis and reaching a conclusion of value. It is all so subjective. That is not to say that we haven't made a great deal of progress with respect to the way we formulate our opinions. We have. But when is it criminal fraud? I mean fraud as in intentionally trying to mislead the reader, investor, or lender by inflating an appraisal.

In the Benny case, even seasoned appraisers were misled by Benny and his associates by receiving corrupt data and sales from the sales office that were not truly arm's length transactions. They were sales that were the result of "straw buyers." This one case (Benny) resulted in the way the secondary market (FNMA and Freddie Mac) dealt with comparable condominium sales on appraisals. First, all sales used in an appraisal from that time on had to be verified with third-party entities, not a developer or real estate agent in the sales office, preferably through county recorders offices or other county records. Second, it was important that at least one to two sales were from nearby competing projects in order to stop developers from "creating a market" similar to what Benny had created at Diamond Heights. In other words, as Benny bought the units using "straw buyers" at fictitious prices, every new sale in the project created a false new value, which, in turn, would be used as a comparable sale to establish a new even higher value in the project. By using outside comparables, this method of inflating values would be restricted.

A number of appraisals are relatively easy to spot for fraud, such as the use of fabricated comparable sales, misleading or omitted data, and even the inclusion of nonexistent improvements. I am sure even photographs have been doctored using software programs such as PhotoShop.

Back in the 1970s, I was accompanying another appraiser who was making a field inspection on a large apartment building. He told me that when inspecting an apartment building while performing an appraisal, to make sure to inspect every room of every unit. As we appraisers use indicators such as price per room, price per unit, and price per square foot, every little nook and cranny could result in higher valuations. This appraiser told me a story about an apartment building owner that had actually placed unit numbers on the doors of closets and laundry rooms in order to fool the appraiser into thinking that were more units than actually existed. This would likely increase the valuation that the appraiser would assign the property.

The complete omission of a detrimental influence is another way for an unscrupulous appraiser to inflate a value or perform a fraudulent appraisal. I have reviewed numerous appraisals where the appraisers actually omitted the fact that a property backed up to a freeway off-ramp or that the property was situated on a heavily traveled street. How about using comparables with sweeping views of the Pacific Ocean to value a home with absolutely no view at all and neglecting to point out this fact on the report?

I once got a call from a mortgage broker about appraising a nearby home. It was situated on my street about two blocks away. I could walk to the property! As I live in a small coastal town of approximately 10,000, about a block from the ocean, I know just about every street in our community. I wondered which property it was. I was told that it was a house, but it was zoned commercial. Since it was so close, I decided to get the mortgage brokers phone number in order to call him back, and ran down the street to take a look at the property. At the end of our street is a small two-story commercial building that includes a small surfboard shop and some office space on both the upper and lower levels. It was not a house, nor had it ever been a house. I called the broker back and told him of my findings. He explained that another appraiser had appraised it earlier as a single-family residence, but that they were unable to locate this particular appraiser in order to get a more recent appraisal. I told him that given the facts as told to me (I did not have an actual appraisal in hand), he was probably dealing with a fraudulent appraisal. For me to call it anything other than what it was (a commercial building), was fraud.

Just to show what a small world this is, an appraiser friend some fifty miles away had received a similar phone call asking for him to appraise the same property. Not only did he get the phone call, but a friend of his received the same phone call asking for an appraisal on this property. This appraisal request sure was getting around.

Requests are made of us every day to "look the other way" with respect to features of properties that lenders might frown upon. For instance, some of the more popular requests are for us to overlook illegal room additions, boot-legged units making the property a multi-family dwelling, leaky roofs, substantial termite damage or dry rot … the list goes on.

Some of these omissions just could be fraud and are rather obvious. What is not so obvious is the selection and use of comparable sales. This is where an enterprising appraiser can fulfill all of the requirements of guidelines set by lenders or secondary markets and can still inflate the value of a property. Using comparable sales in a higher-priced neighborhood than the subject neighborhood is one such trick. A sale could be as close as across the street if the comparable just happens to be situated in a city or town with more "snob appeal" than the subject. A gated community of high-priced homes could be located relatively close by the subject but would be considered, by most, to be a terrible indicator of value if the subject was an older, run-down, ranch-style home of fifty years of age.

Some lenders require that comparable sales be within a certain range with regards to size and/or amenities. If an unscrupulous appraiser utilized sales that fit the lenders guidelines, but were situated in a superior location some distance away, fraud could be the motive.

The FBI recently stated that they have over 1400 cases of mortgage fraud currently under investigation. This seems to me to be a drop in the bucket. As I stated elsewhere, lying on a loan application is fraud.

There are excellent web sites dealing specifically with fraud. One of my favorites is Rachel Dollar's "Mortgage Fraud Blog." Rachel Dollar, the editor of Mortgage Fraud Blog, is an attorney and Certified Mortgage Banker who handles litigation for lending institutions and secondary market investors. She is an author and a nationally recognized speaker on the topic of mortgage fraud. The site can be accessed at http://www.mortgagefraudblog.com and is updated continuously with stories of mortgage fraud from all over the country.

What Goes Up . . .

As we approached the tail end of the 1980s, the real estate market again started to heat up. If there is one thing I have learned from real estate history, it is that markets go up and markets go down. It's cyclical, and nothing can stop these basic economical principles: not economists, the government, or even the powerful National Association of Realtors.

In fact, the market was so heated in 1987–1989 that reading the most recent listings on the local MLS (Multiple Listing Service) was like reading the stock quotes in the Wall Street Journal. Every day the list prices of properties went up, up, up. Although this was to be repeated in the San Francisco Bay Area in the late 1990s, during the dot-com mania and again after the turn of the millennium in 2004–06, it was quite a rise in values at the end of the 1980s.

In May 1989, the floodgates opened, marking an end to the appreciation of home values. In California, and in typical fashion, the San Joaquin Valley was the first to go. It is always the first to go down because it is the last to go up in value. At the end of a rise in a valuation cycle, buyers (especially first-time buyers) are so stretched that they start looking inland, where land is cheaper, thus making housing more affordable. Developers buy up this land on the cheap and build like crazy. The trade-off is commute time, which, in some cases, translates into hours and hours of driving to and from employment each and every day. This grows old.

Areas like Stockton, Modesto, Manteca, Sacramento, Tracy, Brentwood, Oakley, and others always lead the downward spiral. In fact, Stockton is considered ground zero for the current sub-prime mess in Northern California. This same scenario is played out in the high deserts of Southern California in such cities as Victorville, Hesperia, Palmdale, Lancaster, and others.

Eventually, the value erosion hits the Bay Area. It always does. As I stated above, the last real rout came in May, 1989. I would watch the number of listings being put on the local MLS every morning. It started with a handful. Then there would be maybe ten to twelve a day. Soon it became twenty, then forty, a day. After only a couple of months, hundreds of homes were being listed each and every day. This whole event was unfolding before my very eyes. It got to the point where it seemed that every other house was on the market. Each listing placed on the market was priced lower than the listing on the next block or next door- a downward trend not easy to overlook. It was everywhere.

Mortgage brokers would complain that I marked a certain box on the appraisal report labeled "Declining."

What this referred to was an area on the report that described the neighborhood trend with respect to values. Were values increasing, declining, or were they stable? I was told by mortgage broker after mortgage broker that if I checked anything but "Increasing" or "Stable" on the report, they could not broker the loan. The evidence was all around me. There were declining values in one neighborhood after another. I had lost most of my business at the time, as I refused to check any box but the box that stated "Declining Values."

In a rising market, it's difficult to appraise because the comparable sales always lag the market. You are constantly trying to find the most recent sales because the older sales reflect older prices. In a declining market, just the opposite is true- the more recent the sale, the lower the value. That is why real estate agents always bring dated comparable sales to the appraisal inspection in a declining market- they reflect a higher price.

Speaking of real estate agents, there has always been friction between real estate agents and appraisers. This is primarily due to the nature of their occupations. The appraiser is interested in facts. Cold, hard data is at the heart of his/her analysis. The real estate agent mostly deals with emotions. The buyers and sellers are making choices based on needs, wants, circumstances, and preferences.

This puts the two at odds with each other. I can't begin to count the number of times that real estate agents have verbally lambasted me over valuations. I don't understand why they don't know more about the appraisal process. In fact, I don't know why agents don't measure the house they are selling, but they don't. It only takes a few minutes and they are getting paid a lot more than the appraiser to know something about the listing they have. Most claim they don't want the liability of making a mistake, but the reality is that it's not that difficult to measure a house. And besides, that's what Errors & Omissions insurance is for.

We are normally seen as obstacles between the real estate agent and their commission checks, and it's not just real estate agents who have a low opinion of our industry. I was at a small party a few years ago involving the parents of my wife's high school musical students (she was the director). Two dads from totally unrelated industries started talking about appraisers. One made the comment that he never met an appraiser he couldn't sway (with respect to opinion of value) by taking the appraiser to lunch. It was, again, one of those moments that makes your heart sink. This dad was not a "Tony Soprano." He was a former local school-board president and former CEO of a Fortune 500 company.

And the funny thing is that it wasn't always that way. I remember going to a social event or cocktail party in the 1980s and being treated like royalty. Almost every single person in the room wanted to question us. Everybody's house was going up in value and we were almost mysterious to some: How did we value property? How did we learn to appraise? What was my house worth? It was nice.

Easy Money Policies Start an Avalanche

The value erosion in the State of California during the early 1990s was widespread. It affected Northern California as well as Southern California. I have read some accounts lately that values never did go down. This is simply not true. Values statewide went down 20–25 percent in the early 1990s. That represents a down payment in the days before 100 percent financing. In addition, it took approximately eight to ten years for real estate to recover. It always does. This was a typical cycle in length.

This is what amazes me about the current downturn. All of these so-called investors, reporters on the business channel, and newspaper writers are all waiting for the "Housing Bust" to bottom out. It doesn't work that way. It's like waiting for a phone to ring. It just doesn't ring.

Real estate cycles bottom out when the last investor has left town and nobody wants to buy real estate.

As we approached the end of the 1990s, we entered the "dot-com" boom. This was an era of easy and fast money for those that were in the internet business. We all looked around like the world was passing us by and like we were witnessing a new world order. Kids just out of college were making hundreds of thousands of dollars for taking jobs with tech start-up companies. Bonuses consisted of brand new BMWs and stock options.

In fact, stock options played such a large role in the local SF Bay Area economy that even landlords of commercial office space wanted stock options as part of the lease. Eventually, this all spilled over to the residential real estate industry. All of these instant millionaires had to put that money somewhere and boy, did they! They were bidding up the prices of properties and purchasing everything in sight. They would out-bid each other in order to get the property, often by $100,000 or more. The amazing difference between the run-up of values in the dot-com era and that of the 2004–2007 periods is cash. Buyers would put up stock option cash, often times up to 50 percent of the homes purchase price. Contrast that with the 100 percent financing of the 2004–2007 binge.

I remember appraising a property in Portola Valley, a quaint little suburb with mostly horse-type properties on acreages. The buyer paid more than $1,000,000 more than the asking price, but the real shocker was that almost every comparable sale sold for more than $1,000,000 over their respective asking prices! How is an appraiser suppose to estimate what fair market value is under these types of circumstances? Nobody seemed to know the value of a dollar. This scenario was being repeated over and over again until the dot-com bust. By some accounts, we then slipped into a recession. The stock market, especially NASDAQ, crashed. It looked to me as if the boom cycle was over. More and more inventory started showing up on the local MLS, just like in 1989. If that wasn't enough, we then had September 11, which I thought would just sink the real estate market.

One thing I hadn't counted on was Alan Greenspan and his easy money policies. I had been in the business over twenty years up to that point and most of it was spent with interest rates of 9 percent to over 10 percent. Rates fell dramatically in the new millennium and I became increasingly distraught over the way the industry was headed.

Too many people have gotten into the game over the past fifteen years. Did you know that just a couple of years ago there were over 500,000 real estate licensees in the state of California? Some estimates indicate that there over 1,500,000 real estate licenses nationwide, meaning that a third are in California alone. The ranks of appraisers in California swelled from 10,000 to over 22,000.

When I would travel to Palm Springs during the recent boom, the local newspaper was filled with real estate ads. It seemed that every page had houses and condos for sale. Even the front page had a real estate ad on it. There were more pictures of real estate agents than celebrities. Large display ads of realty companies filled magazines and newspapers. Appraisers weren't left out either. A trip to the local grocery store turned up an appraiser advertis-

ing on those little plastic dividers customers use to sepa-
rate their groceries on the conveyor belts. Another had
an "Appraisermobile," an automobile that was painted up
like a moving billboard advertising his services. I'm sure
somewhere in the ads of both was the word "Professional,"
a term that I would not use to describe such methods of
promotion.

Palm Springs wasn't an isolated example. I witnessed
the same thing in Malibu, San Francisco, San Jose, Los
Angeles, and other areas. The real estate business had
become one the largest "carnie acts" I had ever seen! Then
the reality shows on television starting popping up, such
as "Flip This House." It really became a circus atmosphere
and Wall Street participated in a big way. Cheap, easy
money was the rule.

Before long, mortgage brokers had taken over the
business. They began to originate over 70 percent of all
new loans. One of their tactics was to call up an appraiser
and ask for a "comp check." What this amounted to was
an implied opinion of value. It is illegal for a licensed or
certified appraiser to arrive at a "pre-determined" value.
This means an appraiser cannot value a property without
inspecting it, gathering and analyzing sufficient market
data, and arriving at a conclusion of value that is reasonable. What the loan broker wants is the highest value possible. He wants an appraiser to give the broker an estimate
of what he will come in at. Ten appraiser "comp checks"
would mean ten different values. Pick the highest value.
The appraisal industry is mostly to blame for doing these
"comp checks." If every appraiser said no, we wouldn't
have them. I have never met or talked with a loan agent
that didn't say that saving his client money was at the

heart of this whole issue. To that, I say, "If you want to save your client money, throw in part of your commission or steer him away from that sub-prime loan!" Don't expect appraisers to spend a lot of time without being compensated playing your little game of "Dialing for Dollars." What you end up with is the worst of ten opinions of value, not the best. I estimate that the number of comp checks resulting in actual appraisal orders to be somewhere around 1 percent, a figure that may just be high.

Just like in the 1980s, I again became weary of mortgage brokers. In approximately 2003–2004, an appraiser friend and I developed a relationship with World Savings under their WIC (World Independent Contractor) program. We both felt this was a good move, as World's reputation had been made on the quality of their appraisals and ability to really look at the risk of any given property. In fact, this is where they put most of their emphasis over the qualifications of the borrower. They were interested in having independent appraisers handle over-flow work that their own staff appraisers could not handle. I think we were also expected to perform appraisals that some of their own staff didn't have the experience or expertise to perform.

World had both a retail loan department (loans that they originated) and a wholesale loan department (loans that were brokered to them). We did appraisals on both. They would send out a reviewer on almost every appraisal we did, which was fine with me. I have always (since the Benny case) performed every appraisal with the thought of having to defend it on the stand. This, I believe, is a pretty high standard and should be followed by every appraiser. One of the reviewers once told me that she would rather review one of my appraisals than those of the staff appraisers, because I knew exactly what I was doing. It was quite a compliment.

Life was good again. I found a client that wanted good and honest appraisals. They would offer classes to us for continuing education credits. We would even be compensated for "no-shows," appointments where the borrower wouldn't show up for the appointment. I had found a home, but soon enough, the market began to change.

Purchases were becoming more and more difficult to appraise. Fueled by low interest rates, low or no money-down deals, and liar loans (loans that require no verification of income or assets), buyers were out-bidding each other just like in the days of the dot-com boom. The main difference between the markets of the dot-com boom and the market of the 2004–2006 market was cash. The dot-com era produced an enormous number of instant millionaires in the San Francisco Bay Area. Even regular rank and file employees received huge stock options and were swimming in cash. This contrasted with the "no money down" crowd of 2004. "Other People's Money" or OPM, as it is often called, has been the mantra of real estate agents and get-rich-quick gurus over the last thirty years.

Most people don't care what they pay for a property or product if they are not required to put any capital or cash into the deal. This is a fact. I would see this play out over and over again during this period. Borrowers would pay $50,000, $100,000, or even $1,000,000 over the asking price as long as they didn't have to put much cash into the deal. I thought this was insane at the time, and I think it is insane today. On a grand scale, this same principle was being played out on Wall Street by large banks, investment banks, and insurance companies by the large bets they were placing that were often leveraged forty to one. This was a classic example of "Other People's Money"! This leverage is great when things are going up but can be disastrous if things are going south.

There are numerous similarities between the stock market crash of 1929 and the real estate crash of 2007–2010. First, you could buy stock in 1929 on margin meaning you only had to put up 10 percent of the value of the stock and the rest was borrowed money from the brokerage house. Contrast that with the no-money down transactions of the 2004–2006 binges. Talk about leverage and stupid. I don't like that word much, but in this case, the shoe fits. It was stupid for the borrowers to borrow, it was stupid for the lenders to give them the money, and it was stupid for the investors to snatch up all of these toxic debt instruments based on this formula. What were they thinking?

It wasn't enough that World (and others like WAMU) were losing market share to the mortgage brokers; they now had to deal with appraisals that couldn't support the sales prices. In other words, the mortgage brokers could get the job done for the real estate agents and the large lenders could not by using comp checks, etc.

My recollections of the following situation are quite vivid, as it normally takes quite a bit to startle me. World wanted to have a meeting with a large number of their WIC (World Independent Contractors) appraisers. They notified us and it was held in a hotel conference room in Los Gatos, California. There were approximately seventy-five WIC appraisers in the room sitting at tables.

Several World appraisal managers took turns addressing the group. One gentleman was from Texas and his message was this: We are losing market share to the brokers and we want it back.

One of the reasons given for the loss in market share was that appraisals were coming in too low or under the contract price. We were all becoming too conservative. We needed to be more liberal with our valuations- up to 20 percent more liberal. World had no way of competing in the market place if we were going to come in low on appraisals. My friend and I looked at each other in disbelief. Had the fox finally gained entry to the chicken coop at World, too? Were we expected to just arbitrarily add 20 percent to each valuation? Our concern proved to be wasted. Neither of us ever received another purchase appraisal request from World Savings. We did, however, receive refinancing appraisal requests but never a purchase appraisal. I can only assume that staff performed them.

After the turn of the millennium, I was performing a substantial number of appraisals for a mortgage division of a large national bank that is still in existence today. A large number of their loans were being brokered to Washington Mutual, otherwise known as WAMU. WAMU had their own appraisal department at the time and it was one of the most difficult "approved appraiser" lists to get on in the industry. As my client was brokering such a large number of loans to them, it would sure make the process easier for them if I was on that list, making it unnecessary for a review on each and every appraisal I performed for them. The rub was that WAMU was not adding any new appraisers to that list and that policy stood for many years. In fact, it took me many years to finally get on that list, with the help and persistence of my client. But I did get on the list and was assigned a number.

At some point in time, WAMU closed down their appraisal department and started feeding appraisal assignments to EAppraiseit, an AMC. It was this arrangement that finally interested New York Attorney General Andrew Cuomo and started his involvement in the appraisal industry.

As we entered 2006, volume started to dry up, both at World and from other clients. The brokers and Wall Street had taken over the industry and that was that. Soon, World Savings (Golden West) was sold to Wachovia at the absolute peak of the financing binge. This was good news to founders Herb and Marion Sandler, but it turned out to be bad news for Wachovia, its employees, shareholders, its appraisers, and me. By the end of 2008, Wachovia was rescued by white knight Wells Fargo and Co. This was to become a trend in the banking and stock brokerage industries as JP Morgan Chase swallowed up failing Washington Mutual (WAMU), the country's largest savings and loan, and Bank of America purchased Countrywide Mortgage, the country's largest mortgage company, and also Merrill Lynch, the giant stock brokerage firm.

The AMCs Are Driving Seasoned Appraisal Veterans from the Industry

I believe it was in the late 1980s when the AVM (automated valuation model) was first introduced. Here was a product designed to lower the cost of valuations and speed up the process of determining value. It was also capable of performing analysis of entire mortgage pools with respect to valuations. After all, it was in the 1980s when my office was so backed up with appraisal requests that I had to contact the local newspaper for assistance in getting the word out.

This, of course, had a tremendous impact on the appraisal industry. A large number of people predicted the end of the appraiser. Lenders loved the AVM. The most obvious drawback was that they cannot accurately describe or quantify the current condition of the property or site influences that would affect the value (positive or negative). This, in some instances, could make for substantial differences in valuations. For example, what if the subject property backed up to a railroad track or freeway access, or was situated across the street from a firehouse? How about being located on a busy street or adjacent to a high school? I must admit, however, that these same factors could be omitted by an unscrupulous appraiser inflating a value.

The secondary market (FNMA and Freddie Mac) supported and continues to support the new technology, especially in the loan origination process with their automated loan submission products (Loan Prospector and Desktop Underwriter).

There are numerous software companies that have integrated with the various programs and lender networks, all making the process more complex and sophisticated. The shortcomings, as I see it, have always been the assumptions that are made to program the models. I don't think a large number of these programmers have ever been through a down cycle in the real estate market or they would have prepared more for it and programmed some real default scenarios into their projections.

I know one mortgage software developer who has been in the industry since 1998. He has missed all of the major downturns in the past thirty years with the exception of the dot-com bust, which was short-lived (thanks again to Greenspan). His background is in space physics, which is impressive. However, the real estate markets don't always move in predictable ways as an airplane might. He believes that the market will snap back, but my experience of over thirty-five years is that it seldom does. It takes years to restore confidence in the markets.

There is a role for automation. It has improved various tasks for the average appraiser, such as digital photography, data sources like county records and MLS services, aerial photography such as Google Earth, and countless environmental sites that make it easier to evaluate properties and neighborhoods. However, no computer is going to take the place of an experienced and ethical appraiser in the field inspecting the interior and exterior of a structure. Both appraisals and appraisers have gotten better and more detailed over the years, thanks to the continuing education requirements of the various state appraisal licensing departments and the various appraisal organizations. I know my work has improved over the years. I would hate to view one of my early hand-written reports, made so many years ago for The Colwell Company, and have to compare it with an appraisal I have performed in the last couple of years.

There is a trend, however, for large banks to use AMCs (appraisal management companies). These are large appraisal firms that employ typically entry-level appraisers or appraisers with limited experience that will perform appraisals cheaply for access to appraisal business. For example, the typical appraisal fee in Northern California is $350.00 to $400.00 for a tract-like home with no unusual characteristics or components that would make it a complex assignment. It has been this amount for almost ten years. The typical AMC appraiser might receive $175.00 or less for the same assignment. The AMC acts like a middleman, similar to a mortgage broker. These

AMCs are often owned by large title insurance companies or even the mortgage companies or banks themselves.

Most legitimate appraisers who have studied the art of appraising despise these institutions because they attempt to control the process. They lock up a national account such as a large bank or partner with them, offer little in the way of appraisal fees, and leave the door open for abuse, pressure, and influence over the appraisers with respect to values. If you don't "play ball" with them, they can simply take you off their roster.

One of the largest players in the AMC industry is First American Title Company. Through its partnerships with the various lenders and banks, it has firmly established itself as one of the leaders of Appraiser Management Companies.

For example, with its association with Citigroup (Citibank), it has formed the AMC Finiti. With Wells Fargo, it has formed Rels Valuation. With JP Morgan Chase, the AMC is called Quantrix. The partnership with KeyBank is called Secolink. First American Title is not the only title company to partner with a lender. Countrywide formed a subsidiary for its title, settlement, and valuation services called LandSafe.

These AMCs, the lenders argue, create a "firewall" between the loan originator and the appraiser, which, in some form, has been mandated by the HVCC (Home Valuation Code of Conduct). However, there are other consequences of AMCs. In essence, what the AMCs do is establish a rock-bottom appraisal fee that they are willing to pay the appraisers that they contract with for their services and then turn around and bill the lender or client (borrower) the higher market rate for appraisals. What this promotes is the use of less experienced appraisers who will work for peanuts because, for some reason, they are not able to build a client base of their own. This is also a huge profit center for the AMC, bank, or both when times are good as they process thousands of appraisal requests. Do borrowers care that over 50 percent of the appraisal fee that they pay will go to a middleman and not the appraiser that performed the appraisal, or that the fee they pay will not bring the most experienced and highest qualified appraiser to their door? They didn't seem to mind paying all that money to mortgage brokers or middlemen on their loans.

Up until recently, the New York Attorney General Andrew Cuomo and both Fannie Mae and Freddie Mac had agreed, along with their regulators, to create an independent organization to implement and monitor new appraisal standards. I will discuss this in more depth in a later chapter, but there is resistance to some of its policies when it comes to AMCs. What this Cuomo-GSE agreement does is force lenders to use AMCs (some of which are owned in part or whole by the lenders themselves) in order to give the impression that there is a "firewall" between the originator and the appraiser. Mortgage brokers will no longer be able to order the appraisal direct. However, faster than the government can dry the ink on the agreement, new AMCs are appearing on the scene and finding loopholes. One appraiser writes:

> I got an e-mail a few days ago from an AMC company I have never heard of. He stated that if I referred any MBs (mortgage brokers) to him, all I would have to do is let him know that I referred

them and he would be sure I got the order. Has
anyone else received the same e-mail?

So much for "firewall" and for preventing the mortgage
broker from ordering the appraisal directly!

The ranks of AMCs appear to be growing weekly. With
no real oversight or regulation, abuse is all but assured.
Reports are beginning to surface of former appraisers that
have lost their licenses after being sanctioned by state regulatory agencies are now heading up various AMCs. The
same "unscrupulous" sub-prime players and appraisers
that were to partially blame for the mortgage meltdown
in the first place are reportedly setting up shop as AMCs,
according to a Business Week in a February 2009 article.

If that wasn't enough, there are reports by legitimate
and longtime appraisers being removed by AMCs and
banks from AMC approved appraiser lists because they
refuse to perform appraisals and reviews at ridiculously
low fees. Turning in reports past a deadline regardless of
the complexity of the assignment will also get an appraiser
"black-balled" from an approved appraiser list. Seasoned
appraisal veterans are also being black-balled from AMCs
when inexperienced appraisers perform "reviews" of their
work and determine that the report is "wrong" or incor-
rect. In a letter dated April 1, 2008 to the Alabama Attorney General's office, the Alabama Real Estate Appraisers
Board wrote:

> "The HVCC (Home Valuation Code of Conduct),
> as written, harms the very profession it is purported
> to protect. The HVCC is constructed in such a way
> as to inevitably drive the appraisal ordering process
> through appraisal management companies (AMCs).

AMCs generally cut the fees of appraisers, which, in turn, we feel will result in poorer quality appraisals. Because most of the more experienced and highly qualified appraisers will not accept the lower fees, the HVCC will likely force many honest, well-qualified appraisers out of the business." The letter goes on to say: "It is the belief of the Alabama Real Estate Appraisers Board that the HVCC, as it is currently written, will have a negative effect on the integrity of the appraisal process and further erode the public trust in the appraisal process."

Another state board, the Nebraska Real Property Appraiser Board, in a letter dated May 2008, wrote,

There are no agencies that monitor or regulate such entities (AMCs) and yet they are responsible for the valuation of thousands of appraisal reports on a daily basis. As is evidenced by the EAppraisit, Washington Mutual Case, Appraisal Management Companies have not always acted as disinterested third parties providing independent valuation services. In the referenced case, abuses reportedly have included "pushing" appraisers by threatening to cease doing business if certain values were not met.

Cash flow continues to be the primary motivation of AMCs. Cash flow is typically accomplished at the expense of appraisal quality by "squeezing" the individual appraiser through fee reduction, unreasonable turn times, or both. Due to the lack of adequate time and compensation, the appraiser is compelled to generate a work product that received very little consideration in terms of due diligence. Such appraisal products were regularly delivered to the secondary market as compliant reports.

Appraisers need adequate time and compensation to perform work that is compliant with the Uniform

Standards of Professional Appraisal Practice (USPAP). While AMCs will argue that decisions made by individual appraisers are 'business decisions,' no one can argue the fact that AMCs use unreasonable leverage in their dealings by making apparent their national or regional client relationships and the amount of appraisal work that they can disburse to individual appraisers. In many cases, these AMCs control the market and use that leverage unfairly.

That's quite an indictment, coming from an appraisal oversight agency, but one that is shared by many.

The Department of Business and Industry's Real Estate Division for the State of Nevada writes, in a letter dated April 23, 2008:

Although there will undoubtedly be unforeseen ramifications and unintended consequences of this agreement that can only be addressed as they emerge, at the outset, we are very concerned about including appraisal management companies (AMCs) and correspondent lenders among those who are impartial and unbiased when it comes to the appraisal process. In our experience, the opposite is often the case. AMCs need to perform well for their clients; and some elements of that performance test are turn-around time, frequency of "call backs," competitive fees, and quantity of successful transactions.

In practice, there is really very little difference between correspondent lenders and mortgage bankers or brokers. Simply put, they are third party originators. Currently, the lender may transfer the origination of loans to a third party, but, in practice, that does not transfer the lender's responsibility for the quality of such loans to another party. Some third parties will inevitably have other motivations that overshadow their concern about the quality of the loans.

Our major concerns are two-fold: there is insufficient funding at the state level to enforce the existing laws, and if AMCs and correspondent lenders are left in the mix of those who are to impartially orchestrate the appraisal process, the next bridge we must cross is how to regulate them.

There also seems to be an interest of attorneys in going after the AMCs and banks that are affiliated with them. In a recent press release noted on MarketWatch.com, Hagens Berman Sobol Shapiro, a Seattle, Washington based law firm is "investigating Wells Fargo and their appraisal subsidiary Rels Valuation, based on reports the companies allegedly engaged in a rigged appraisal process designed to boost profits at the expense of homeowners and independent appraisers."

On another press release by Hagens Berman:

A group of Washington homeowners this week filed a lawsuit against Countrywide, a wholly owned subsidiary of Bank of America and the nation's largest mortgage company, claiming the mortgage giant illegally rigged the appraisal process in a scheme to boost profits at the expense of homeowners and independent appraisers. The lawsuit claims LandSafe subcontracts much of its appraisal work to a network of independent appraisers, but offers them rates as low as $140 per appraisal. The company then marks the costs of the appraisal back as high as $410 when invoicing homeowners.

The Nebraska Real Property Appraiser Board asserts:

> Essentially, Appraisal Management Companies are free to act as they please without any oversight or regulatory scrutiny. The substandard appraisal products are, in this board's opinion, the direct result of the actions and behaviors exhibited by the unregulated Appraisal Management Companies.

The Arizona Board of Appraisal puts it another way:

> The Board urges that the ramifications of using appraisal management companies be carefully considered. It has been the Board's experience that complaints regarding appraisal management companies are not subject to any oversight or regulation. To that end, the Board is concerned that the integrity of the primary and secondary markets will not improve if current practices by these companies do not change. The focus of these companies appears to be primarily speed and cost with little or no emphasis on quality of the appraisal or experience and competence of the appraiser. To ensure a greater emphasis on a quality product to restore public trust, it is imperative that appraiser management companies be regulated, either federally or required of all states at the state level.

My only problem with their position comes in the last sentence "...companies be regulated..." As you will see in a later chapter, both the feds and states have a difficult time overseeing individual appraisers. I doubt that they will have the resources to oversee large national AMCs. The business model for AMCs just doesn't serve the need of the public trust.

If that wasn't enough of an argument against AMCs, there was this little gem about the AMCs that caught more than a few appraisers eye. A few years ago, a local bay area newspaper wrote an article on a national AMC out-sourcing their appraisal reviews to India. This brought up numerous questions, the least of which was about privacy issues relating to sensitive financial data pertaining to borrowers and their properties in the hands of individuals overseas.

David Lazarus, then with the San Francisco Chronicle and now with the Los Angeles Times, wrote in 2004:

> If you owned a million-dollar home, not a terribly far-fetched notion in these parts, would you want your name, address, and residential details being sent abroad for examination by foreign clerical workers? Probably not. But homeowners who refinanced their mortgages with Citigroup may indeed have had their property appraisals outsourced to India as part of efforts by the financial-services giant to cut costs and streamline its loan process.

A spokeswoman with Citigroup replied, "We do it with the basic first-level review to make sure the appraisal is in order."

I was shocked when this story broke and I am really appalled after reading a recent Wall Street Journal headline outlining how the chairman of a giant outsourcing company in India had resigned and been arrested after he admitted to "cooking the books" for years. This came just weeks after the revelation that Bernard Madoff had engineered a giant, fifty-billion dollar Ponzi scheme that lasted decades. Who can we trust? It all comes down to "due diligence."

Scott Woolley wrote an article about the title insurance business in a 2006 article for Forbes Magazine. In the article, Mr. Woolley pointed out that the title insurance industry brings in over $18 billion a year for a product that is largely outdated, loosely regulated, is protected by law against competition, and rarely pays a claim for title fraud or hidden liens. The business has not only quadrupled in ten years, but has seen their average charge double to $1,472 per home for a title search and insurance. Woolley asserts,

> Meanwhile, thanks to computerized record-keeping, the cost of searching for a home's ownership records online has fallen to as low as $25. Technology also has helped make mistakes rarer; now only $74 of each policy goes to pay claims- that is, make buyers with defective deeds whole. That leaves a $1,473 spread for overhead and for profit.

There have been numerous lawsuits against title companies for paying kickbacks to real estate agents, lenders, and others in order to attain larger market share.

One such lawsuit brought by the Commissioner of the State of California resulted in First American very quietly agreeing to pay more than $10 million in fines to settle charges that it had engaged in illegal kickbacks in exchange for referral of business. Says Woolley,

> Now some forces are working to rein in this rapacious industry. Officials in dozens of counties are working to standardize home-ownership for digital access by the public. The U.S. Department of Housing &

Urban Development is mulling over ways to force more competition on the industry, though previous efforts have failed utterly.

Jeff Schurman is a pitchman for the TAVMA (Title/Appraisal Vendor Management Association), which promotes the vendor management industry and "presents its members'" positions to government and media, protects its members' rights to do business without unfair and anti-competitive legislation and regulations, and provides useful information about issues impacting the real estate settlement services industry."

He blogs that:

1. Most residential appraisers work with AMCs, or have worked with at least one in the last five years, disputing the notion that only a small cabal of lousy appraisers does AMC work.

2. The majority of appraisers who do not work with AMCs would do so if they were to earn higher fees, confirming that it's all about the money.

3. Each appraiser who works with an AMC agrees up front to the expectations regarding quality, service, and fees, evidence that appraisers who work with AMCs do so of their own free will.

4. The assertion that you get what you pay for when it comes to AMC appraisals is unfounded; AMCs give back something

of value to appraisers in return for the
appraisers best pricing.

Is it simply a matter of appraisal costs and of who will
perform them the cheapest. As I have outlined before,
the ongoing education and experience of an appraiser is
expensive and paramount to a good, quality appraisal.
The costs don't end there, however. We, as independent
fee appraisers, must carry Error & Omissions insurance,
the cost of data (such as MLS services, title data, county
records data, etc.) continues to rise as does the cost of
transporting ourselves to the property, the health care of
our family and ourselves continuing to escalate, and we
are constantly keeping up with the Jones's with respect to
technology and software. The cost of renewing our state
certification is $435.00 vs. the cost of renewal for a real
estate broker of $165.00. And to compound this, we are
losing business to Automated Valuation Models, Broker
Price Opinions, and entry level appraisers who work for
Appraisal Management Companies. Is it any wonder we
feel like the milkman when it comes to possible extinction?

Conflicts of Interest

Going back as far as I can remember, I've always had a problem with conflicts of interest. It started with what I thought was an obvious conflict: that of a real estate agent representing both the buyer and seller in a real estate transaction. Here in California, according to law, all agents have a "fiduciary" responsibility to their client in a transaction. If this is true, how can an agent represent both parties in a transaction and still keep this fiduciary relationship intact? I know the realtors say that the buyer can sign a "buyer's broker agreement" with their agent, but what about a case with an absence of such an agreement? In the California Department of Real Estate "Real Estate Bulletin" (Summer 2007, Pg 1), Wayne S. Bell, Chief Counsel, writes:

> Fiduciary duties impose the highest standard of care, and real estate licensees must be committed to scrupulously fulfilling those obligations. California law imposes the following fiduciary duties on real

estate licensees: To exercise the utmost honesty, absolute candor, integrity, and unselfishness toward the client requires that an agent not compete with his or her client and act, at all times, in the best interest of his or her client to the exclusion of all other interests, including interests that could benefit the agents or others. In addition, this requires that a licensee refrain from dual representation in a real estate sales transaction unless he or she obtains the consent of both principals after full disclosure.

The conflicts are everywhere. A few years ago, I was performing a review appraisal on another appraisers report. As this was a field review, I was to perform a "drive-by" review of the subject property. You can imagine my surprise when I noticed the appraisers name on the sold sign: Sold By _____. I also had a signed copy of the sales contract with me and found the appraiser's brother also acting as one of the agents involved. He turned out to be unlicensed. After reviewing the report, I concluded the sales price had been inflated and the loan was turned down. I also submitted the report to the Department of Real Estate Appraisers in Sacramento, where the gentleman was already under investigation.

Some conflicts are obvious, like the above example. Others are not so obvious. Take, for example, my dealings with a number of banks and mortgage companies over the years. These large institutions hire loan officers or loan representatives. These individuals are employees of the bank or mortgage company, but often times are allowed to select the appraiser they use in a transaction. Again, if the appraiser continues to value the properties for less than the sales price or less than the borrower needs to conclude the transaction, the loan agent will simply stop using the appraiser and start working with another. In this business, you are only as good as your last high appraisal.

Value is not always the issue, either. On one occasion, I was requested to appraise a property and was asked by the owner to meet him for the inspection at a certain time. I agreed and arrived at the property a few minutes early. After knocking on the door, I was greeted by a gentleman who told me he was the tenant and agreed to let me in to start the inspection of the home. The owner arrived a few minutes later and insisted he was the occupant. After seeing the tenant's clothes in the closet, along with his other personal belongs all over the house, it was difficult to believe the owner's statements about living in the house. I correctly checked the "tenant occupied" box on the form. After turning in the report, I was called by the loan agent and told that I had made a mistake. I explained what had happened, but to no avail. He tried to provide me with documentation to prove his client lived there. He provided no drivers license, no voter's registration card, no passport, no income tax return, or any similar documents, just a utilities bill that went to that address. Why am I concerned so much with an owner's occupancy? It's because the borrower can qualify for a more favorable rate when the property is owner-occupied. And in this case, the borrower was trying to qualify for a line of credit or home equity loan, only available for owner-occupied properties. Lying on a loan application is fraud, no matter how you look at it. Lying about occupancy or lying about income, it's all the same: fraud. Because of my failure to "play ball," I lost another client or loan officer and never received another appraisal request from that gentleman.

After witnessing the World Savings request for what I found to be arbitrarily higher values, and the fact that, at most major lenders, the loan officer had the ability to control the selection of the appraiser, I am convinced that any relationship a bank, savings and loan, or mortgage company has with an appraiser or appraisal firm has to be even more than arm's length or the appearance of arm's length. There must be a "firewall" between the lender and the appraiser.

Most of these lenders are not around anymore or, at the least, have become taken over by a more healthy institution, including very large stalwarts such as World Savings (becoming Wachovia and then being taken over by Wells Fargo), Washington Mutual, Countrywide Financial, Bear Sterns, Merrill Lynch, and even Fannie Mae and Freddie Mac.

If there are to be unbiased, objective appraisals, there must be protection from outside influences and threats of lost employment or revenue. Having a lender partially own, or partner with, a title company in an AMC is not a firewall. Real estate companies that own or control a mortgage company is another obvious conflict of interest and most of the real estate companies (both large and small) have mortgage company divisions. Developers and builders that have subsidiaries such as a mortgage company is another obvious conflict. There is too much faith being given to these industries. Again, it is the fox and the chicken coop.

Even Alan Greenspan recently admitted before Congress that he had been wrong to think banks' ability to assess risk and their self-interest would protect them from excesses (Wall Street Journal, Kara Scannell and Sudeep Reddy, Pg 1, 10/24/08). Interestingly enough, Mr. Greenspan answered questions about falling home prices: "I did not forecast a significant decline in home prices because we had never had a significant decline in home prices." I wonder where Mr. Greenspan was during 1989–1991.

The credit rating agencies such as Standard & Poor's, Moody's, and Fitch also present an interesting set of conflicts. These three agency's are paid to rate financial instruments produced by the very same people that pay to rate them. If an agency won't give a certain bond or pool of mortgages a favorable rating, the broker or investment banker will simply go to someone else who will, for a price, give them a favorable rating. It's like the "comp check" discussed earlier. You end up with the least reliable rating or value when it is based on "dialing for dollars" instead of a well thought out analysis of the asset.

Again, a "firewall" is needed between the rating agency and the company that requests the rating. Isn't this just plain common sense? This firewall is probably a good idea for bank examiners and accounting firms that provide auditing services to major corporations, too. Shouldn't someone working for Arthur Andersen, the former giant accounting firm, have blown the whistle on Enron, WorldCom, and themselves? This issue of rubber-stamping appraisals, audits, and investment ratings really annoys me to no end. These large corporations are not too big to fail, either. Arthur Andersen folded the tent after their conviction, even though the conviction was overturned by the Supreme Court years later. Who would want the Arthur Andersen name on their company's audit and annual report? Yet we bailout companies like AIG, the giant insurance company, because they were greedy and failed to realize the inherent risk in insuring bonds backed by toxic mortgages. This attitude of "too big to fail" must be re-examined. If we really must go down this road, it only makes sense to prevent them from getting this big.

We will have to wait and see what the eventual outcome will be for Moody's, Standard & Poor's, and Fitch. What municipality or pension fund can rely on their rating services knowing that the rating may well be based on fees paid to them and not an unbiased analysis of the financial instrument being rated? This is a lot more than just a simple rating. Municipalities use these ratings to help issue bonds in the marketplace that enable them to build schools, construct or improve roadways, expand sewer capacity, fund redevelopment, and so on. These ratings are crucial in attracting capital. They are also used in determining whether a certain financial instrument is "Investment Grade," or suitable for pension funds (both private and public). Municipalities, corporations, and even schools districts use these ratings to determine if certain money pools are safe to park excess operating capital. These rating companies owe it to the public trust to be unbiased in their assessments, as do appraisers and auditors.

Cast of Characters

What has always amazed me about mortgage industry is how many people or corporations want into the business at some point. It really is like the movie industry in that sense (without the glamour).

I discussed earlier about my employment with the Colwell Company in Los Angeles in the 1970s. Not long after I left, the company was purchased by The Baldwin Piano Company. That's right, a piano company. That is not as strange as it seems. Many years ago, Weyerhaeuser, the large forest products company, also got into the mortgage business. It sold the division in 1997, but continues to operate its real estate division that includes home building.

Ford Motor Company entered the business with their ownership of First Nationwide Bank. They were a major player for a number of years. However, in 1994, they exited the business when they sold First Nationwide to Ronald Perleman, the billionaire turnaround artist.

Another aspect of the industry that has always interested me was the type of personalities drawn into real estate, whether it's brokerage or finance. I already mentioned Dr. Christensen and George Benny, both pretty high-profile examples (especially Benny). Over the past thirty-five years, there have been so many more that I have come across.

Take for example, Joe P., a mortgage broker in the San Jose, California, area in the mid-1980s. Joe came from the real estate industry and knew every trick in the book. I was performing appraisals for his small company, but I always watched my back. Joe would run up quite a bill, and then use payment as leverage to try to influence appraisers. Well, he had run up quite a few appraisal fees with my firm and I needed to find a way to get paid.

Performing the actual appraisal is only part of the job. Underwriters like to "condition" loan files and especially appraisals. What this means is that an underwriter may want an appraiser to make a few comments about something in the report. For example, he or she may be asked to elaborate on the condition of one of the comparable sales used in the report or on why no adjustments were made. The appraiser may be asked to correct a mistake found in the report. There are all kinds of reasons for "conditions."

Having a "condition" in hand from a mortgage banker that was funding Joe's loans, I made a phone call to the chief underwriter at the mortgage banker. It turns out that I knew the chief underwriter and told her my problem. She didn't like the idea of this leverage over appraisers any more than I did. She started to "condition" poor Joe's loans prior to his commission checks being drawn. The condition amounted to showing proof that the appraiser (me) was being paid. They would fund the loans but hold Joe's commission checks until he paid down the appraisal fees that he owed me and that were on a list that I had supplied the lender. Joe was none too happy with me, but it just goes to show you to what lengths an honest appraiser has to go to get paid sometimes. He or she shouldn't have to.

Another way for appraisers to put pressure on deadbeat mortgage brokers is to threaten to go to the Department of Real Estate over their record-keeping of clients trust funds. I learned early on to make a copy of every check I receive when I make a deposit. I still do. If I had a problem collecting fees from a lender or broker (assuming it wasn't the first fee), I would go through the copies of deposits to see if a previous check was drawn on a trust account, which was often the case. You see, when Joe the Broker collects the appraisal fee from the borrower, he normally puts it in a trust account. These funds are supposed to be spent on behalf of the borrower and Joe the Broker is required to account for every penny. That includes the appraisal fee. A visit from the Department of Real Estate to look over trust accounts is not a pleasant experience. From the previous check comes all the information you need to start the ball rolling: the account name and, most importantly, the account number. Joe the Broker will usually fall right in line with that threat.

My underwriter friend and I started to perform a little background check on Joe. We found that he was operating on a restricted real estate license. Most of this information is public knowledge and available through the Department of Real Estate in Sacramento. We also found out that his license was restricted because of a felony conviction in another state. It clearly states that real estate agents must be honest and not crooks ... how is it that he still had a license?

Was this just an isolated incident or something that happens just in California? I don't think so. A recent article in the Miami Herald written by Jack Dolan, Rob Barry, and Matthew Haggman explains: "During Florida's housing boom, state regulators allowed thousands of mortgage professionals with criminal records into the industry- costing consumers millions." The newspaper conducted an exhaustive study over an eight-month investigation and analyzed computer records of over 222,844 Florida mortgage professionals, poured over thousands of records from regulators, and reviewed hundreds of court files. What they found was startling:

> From 2000 to 2007, regulators allowed at least 10,529 people with criminal records to work in the mortgage profession. Of those, 4,065 cleared background checks after committing crimes that state law specifically requires regulators to screen, including fraud, bank robbery, racketeering and extortion. More than half the people who wrote mortgages in Florida during that period were not subject to any criminal background check. Despite repeated pleas from industry leaders to screen them, Florida regulators have refused. Regulators allowed at least twenty brokers to keep their licenses even after committing the one crime that seemed sure to get them banned from the industry: mortgage fraud.

I guess you could say that not much has changed since my days with Joe the Broker. In fact, things have gotten worse.

The Savings and Loan Debacle Changed Everything

(Or did it?)

As I explained before, prior to the Savings and Loan debacle of the 1980s, there was no such thing as a real estate appraiser's license. The cost for de-regulating the lending industry was passed on to "Joe the Taxpayer," as it would also be in 2008. We are still paying for that mess, as it quite simply became part of our national debt.

In 1987, nine appraisal organizations (including eight from the U.S. and one from Canada) formed an Ad-Hoc Committee to develop professional standards that would eventually become the Uniform Standards of Professional Appraisal Practice (USPAP). This USPAP was created with the express purpose of promoting and preserving public trust in professional appraisal practice. Congress contributed to USPAP's acceptance by identifying USPAP as the generally recognized standards of practice in the appraisal profession, as did the Executive Branch, Office of Management and Budget (OMB), and private industry groups such as Fannie Mae, Freddie Mac, and others. The key here is "promoting and preserving public trust." As stated in the Appraisal Foundations National USPAP course, "The concept of trust obligates the appraiser to act in the public's interest."

The Financial Institutions Reform, Recovery and Enforcement Act of 1989 (FIRREA) was signed into law by President George H. W. Bush in the wake of the savings and loan crisis of the 1980s. In addition to creating new deposit insurance funds, abolishing existing funds, such as the Federal Savings and Loan Insurance Corporation (FSLIC), moving regulatory authority around (authority from the Federal Home Loan Bank Board (FHLBB) to the Office of Thrift Supervision (OTC), creating the Resolution Trust Corporation (RTC), establishing new capital reserve requirements, and allowing bank holding companies to acquire thrifts, it also established the Appraisal Subcommittee (ASC). This ASC was set up to consist of designees of the heads of the Federal financial institutions regulatory agencies. ASC was also established to adopt appraisal standards for real estate appraisal and enable states to form regulatory agencies to oversee the certification and licensing of individuals who are qualified to perform appraisals on federally related transactions. The ASC was also charged with maintaining a national registry of State certified and licensed appraisers who are eligible to perform appraisals in federally related transactions.

An important aspect of the clean-up was the formation of various departments of real estate appraisers in almost every state. The name of that department here in California is known as OREA (Office of Real Estate Appraisers). Their function is to regulate, qualify, and enforce the laws pertaining to appraisers. They also set up the various educational requirements and make the necessary changes when laws or regulations change.

There are minimum educational and experience requirements to acquiring an appraiser's license, as with most licenses. These requirements are constantly being modified and normally made more difficult and challenging as time goes by.

For example, a Certified Residential License now requires two-hundred hours of education covering ten modules, including a fifteen-hour National USPAP course and an Associate Degree. In lieu of a degree, twenty-one semester credits in specific subject matters may be substituted. The applicant must also have a minimum 2,500 hours encompassing at least thirty months of acceptable experience. For a Certified General License, three-hundred hours of education covering ten modules, including a fifteen hour National USPAP course and a Bachelor's Degree are required. In lieu of a degree, thirty semester credits in specific subject matters may be substituted. The experience requirement for this classification is a minimum 3,000 hours encompassing at least thirty months of acceptable experience. At least 1,500 hours of the experience must be non-residential.

Now let's contrast that with the requirements of a real estate salesman license in the state of California. You must be eighteen years of age or older to be issued a license. You must provide proof of legal presence in the United States. Applicants must be honest and truthful. Conviction of a crime may result in the denial of a license. Failure to disclose any criminal violation or disciplinary action in an applicant's entire history may also result in the denial of a license.

The educational requirement is that the successful completion of three college-level courses is required to qualify for a real estate salesperson examination:

1.   Real Estate Principles

2.   Real Estate Practice

3.   One course from the following list:

> Real Estate Appraisal, Property Management, Real Estate Finance, Real Estate Economics, Legal Aspects of Real Estate, Real Estate Office Administration, General Accounting, Business Law, Escrows, Mortgage Loan Brokering and Lending, Computer Applications in Real Estate, or Common Interest Developments.

Three courses and a promise to be honest? What about my old friend Joe P., the convicted felon?

Both the real estate license and the appraiser license require continuing education. The appraiser license requires proof of successful completion of the seven-hour National USPAP Update course taken within the license term. In addition to the National USPAP Update course, fourteen hours of continuing education is required for each calendar year in which a license is valid (or fifty-six hours every four years).

All real estate brokers and salespersons must complete forty-five clock hours of DRE-approved continuing education (over a four year period) consisting of *either* twelve hours of continuing education courses in the following subjects: (Ethics, Agency, Trust Fund Handling, and Fair Housing) *or* one six-hour course that covers the four mandatory subjects (Ethics, Agency, Trust Fund Handling, and Fair Housing), one three-hour course in Risk Management, and at least eighteen clock hours of consumer protection courses, and the remaining clock hours required to complete the forty-five hours of continuing education may be related to either consumer service or consumer protection courses.

You can see that the experience and educational requirements for an appraiser far out-weight the requirements for a real estate salesman license. However, in most cases, real estate licensees and mortgage brokers reap huge commissions compared to the fee that a typical appraiser might receive. Yet, the price of a certified appraisal is evidently too high and the wait too slow for a large number of lenders, mortgage brokers, and bank REO departments.

The typical appraisal fee on a single family residence was approximately $300 to $400 for a standard tract house and had been for about ten years. As a matter of fact, the pressure on appraisal fees is downward with the proliferation of AMCs and the use of BPOs (Broker Price Opinions).

So with all these mandated experience and educational requirements necessary to not only acquire an appraiser's license, but to keep one, you would think everything was established, wouldn't you? Well, you'd be dead wrong. Somehow, somewhere, the idea was hatched that real

estate agents would be better educated and gain better experience with the valuation process and that they
should be the ones to value property. That's right, brokers
and agents, or "salesmen," would be cheaper and faster
at assigning values. Notice I didn't say "Appraising" or
"Appraised Value." That, as it turns out, is a critical dis-
tinction. I discussed the matter with an investigator with
the OREA (Office of Real Estate Appraisers), the chief
regulator of appraisers in California, and he stated that
if the wording "Appraised Value" or "Appraise" should
be mentioned, a state licensed appraiser must sign it off
and the report must comply with USPAP. If the word
"Appraise" or any derivative is not used, a real estate broker or agent may offer an opinion of value. You have got
to be kidding! After thirty-five years of experience, countless courses, seminars, tests, renewals, etc., I have to compete with a salesman with no prior experience, who passed
a simple test, was at least eighteen years of age, and swore
that he or she was not a crook? A salesman can offer an
opinion of value that a lender can use to dispose of an
REO, make a loan, or extend credit? Even the FDIC uses
BPOs instead of appraisals when valuing REOs for dis-
position on behalf of taxpayers. This was brought to light
by the investigator with the OREA. He said he was told
by employees of the FDIC working on the IndyMac situation that they are using BPOs instead of appraisals and
will only use an appraiser when they think that they may
be positioning themselves to go after his or her E & O
insurance.

Excuse me for thinking that the appraiser is going
the way of the milkman, but there is good reason and
evidence for this. If the creation of the AVM didn't fin-

ish us off, this latest instrument just might. Although it has been around for a long time, the BPO (Broker Price Opinion) has recently become popular for its low cost and alternative to an appraisal. Why there are so many people intent on putting us out of business is beyond me, but that's the way it looks. These BPOs are prepared by real estate brokers or salesmen and not by licensed or certified appraisers. In fact, they can't be performed by appraisers because they would violate guidelines set by the Uniform Standards of Professional Appraisal Practice or USPAP.

Numerous appraisers have mentioned the large number of REOs (Real Estate Owned or bank owned properties) being placed on the market. What is surprising is that real estate agents are performing the BPOs in order to get the listings. As one appraiser asked, "Can't anyone see the inherent conflicts of agents valuing their own listings?" And what's even more troubling is that often times the agent prices the property too low, resulting in lower prices for the lender or investor and even lower values in the subject neighborhoods. As these properties sell, they become the latest comparable in the neighborhood used as a basis for comparison for other appraisals and listings.

Another appraiser states:

> Well, all I can say is they are losing money left and right. I'm guessing that 80 percent of the REO purchase loans I review have appraisals with market values 10 to 15 percent higher then what the property sells for. The BPOs are costing the lenders money and either they don't know or don't care.

A Certified Residential Appraiser in Florida has a different experience with BPOs and writes:

I just picked up a new REO client. My contact is an agent that currently has over a hundred REO properties. I called her to set up two appointments. I called the number on a Saturday and she answered the phone. We got to talking for a while and she said she has been begging this company to use an appraiser. The new client got my number from another client. She said the BPOs she sees are crap. The realtor doing the BPO is asking her for directions, for comps (comparables), and a repair list. She said that a majority come in way too high and she ends up having to sit on the property because the realtors doing these have no idea how to price a BPO. She also told me the company was ordering three to four BPOs on a property and the values were so far apart they were having problems pricing the home. She then says you get what you pay for. She told me the agent was getting fifty bucks a BPO and just pumping them out and not taking the time to understand the market.

And most troubling of all, this appraiser states:

Just found a comp (comparable) for an REO that I'm doing. Realtor did BPO and listed the property at $75k. (no idea if an appraisal was done in conjunction with this). Listing sat on market six months then sold for $20k. Re-listed three days later at $50k. Guess who bought the property for $20k.

These BPOs are gaining market share in the industry because of speed and low cost. Try asking a taxpayer what he would rather have: a thorough, well thought-out opinion of value or a cheap and quick BPO.

I recently came across a definition of an appraisal in an old textbook I was using for research on appraising in the 1970s for this book.

Professional appraisals are more than opinions. They require selective research into appropriate market areas: assemblage of pertinent data, the application of appropriate analytical techniques, and the knowledge, experience, and professional judgment necessary to develop a conclusion that is appropriate to the problem.

Professional judgment is a critical factor. Although a scientific method is applied throughout the appraisal process, appraising is not an exact science. The making of a judgment in the formulation of a conclusion is based on and supported by facts developed from research. The competent appraiser gathers and selects relevant information, applies expertise to the processing of the information, maintains complete objectivity and high ethical standards, and develops a valid conclusion.

In forming the conclusion, the appraiser recognizes and clearly identifies the difference among personal opinions, observed facts, and professional judgments. An estimation of market value reflects market attitudes and actions; personal positions are out of place. (The Appraisal of Real Estate Seventh Edition prepared by the Textbook Revision Subcommittee American Institute of Real Estate Appraisers 1978)

This is not just a question of lost income to appraisers. There are some real consequences resulting from salesmen performing valuations. I can't begin to tell you how many times over the years a real estate agent has mentioned how difficult the appraisal portion of their educational requirements was to grasp.

Enforcement of Existing Regulations

As I stated in the previous chapter, The Savings & Loan fiasco changed everything. One thing that we know it did was establish regulations governing appraisers and their methods. The new regulators were individual offices set up and controlled by each state to oversee and license appraisers in their respective state pursuant to federal mandates.

The latest count of appraisers nationally is estimated at 95,000. Since it's inception in the early 1990s, the roster of appraisers in California averaged approximately 10,000 appraisers. After 2000, the roster had swelled to over 22,000 appraisers statewide. It has since been reduced to 17,300, but that is still a lot of appraisers to regulate with a small staff of clerical workers and investigators. Contrast that with numbers in other states: Nebraska, 907; Missouri, 1,913; Michigan, 6,011; and Arizona, 3,030.

Even though the majority of states have appraiser licensing, surprisingly, there are eight states that don't, according to a recent six-month investigation conducted by the Associated Press. The investigation found that many state appraisal boards and the federal agency tasked with their oversight are understaffed with many having only one investigator to handle hundreds of cases per year and several state boards that don't even have the one investigator. So, how serious are the States and Federal regulators when it comes to oversight of the industry? Evidently, they are not very serious.

When doing review appraisals for a well-known national bank several years ago, I started turning appraisers into the state that were not only incompetent but, in my opinion, were deceitful and fraudulent. On one occasion, I reviewed an appraisal performed on a single-family residence where the appraiser had used town-homes overlooking the Pacific Ocean as a basis for comparison. Never mind that the subject property had no view. The discipline ending up being a "talking to" from the investigator, which brought a promise never to do it again. Most violators are required to take yet more classes in USPAP, as if it was a question of not understanding the standards and guidelines, as opposed to inflating the value of a given property.

According to the AP report, the Appraisal Subcommittee is supposed to help states remove from the system those appraisers who agree to "hit a number." But the

ASC only has four employees to conduct field reviews and audits of fifty states and four U.S. Territories and didn't have a permanent director from late in 2007 (when a previous director retired) until March 2009. And this pretty much mirrors the current status at the state level. Most states are years behind in their investigations and some, like New Hampshire, have decided to close all outstanding files dating to 2002, some of which included allegations of fraud, because they were too old to investigate, according to the AP report. Federal law requires all states to investigate and resolve complaints against appraisers within a year. AP also reports that the only tool federal regulators have to force states into compliance is so severe, that it would effectively halt all mortgage lending in a particular state. This involves a death sentence known as "non-recognition," a penalty that would ban all appraisers in that state from handling deals involving a federal agency or almost all mortgage lending activity.

So, according to the AP report: "Without the ability to issue fines or impose a less destructive punishment, The Appraisal Subcommittee is powerless. It has never taken an action against a state for not obeying the law." To me, it's like California passing the law that prohibits drivers from talking on their cell phones (hands-free phones are exempt). Nobody that I see doing so gets a ticket and it appears that one out of ten drivers still has their cell phone to their ears as they drive. The penalty in California for the first time offender is a whopping twenty dollars. Contrast this with throwing a piece of trash out the window of a moving vehicle; the penalty is $1,000.00. If you want compliance, make the penalty stiff, whether it's trash, cell phones, or mortgage fraud.

Looking at the Mortgage from the Viewpoint of the Investor

We typically associate "flip-flopping" with bad politicians. I think it can be used in a more constructive way. For instance, when I have a particularly difficult piece to play on the piano or the trumpet, I often start in the middle or end of a musical piece and work backwards. This seems to free me up and I can look at the piece from a different point of view. Instead of playing the first measure, then the second, and the third, I will start with the tenth measure, then play the ninth, then the eighth, and so on.

This also works with writing. When I get "writer's block" and can't seem to move on past a certain spot, I step back and start writing a completely different paragraph with a totally dissimilar subject matter or topic.

My point here is to look at the credit crisis from a different point of view in order to help bring back confidence to the market place. Most of the headlines and analysis have been focused on what to do with all of the toxic loans that were made. Who will hold them, purchase them, and sell them? Emphasis is also placed on their worth, whose balance sheet they will end up on, and how to deal with the massive amount of defaults. There is also the finger pointing: Whose fault is this mess, the mortgage brokers, the credit rating agencies, the banks, the borrowers? The list goes on and on. But how do we solve this problem and prevent it from happening again?

Let's flip it over and look at it from a different point of view. If you were an investor in mortgages or mortgage-backed securities today, what would you be looking at in terms of loan quality? First off, you would not be looking for "Liar-loans" or low-documentation loans. You want to be sure that every claim of income or assets can be proven with a reasonable amount of documentation.

Second, you want some "Skin-in-the-game," or a down payment or sufficient equity. How do we know if there is sufficient equity? We already know that computer models are useful, but we also realize that a lot of these projections were way off and caused a great deal of this mess in the first place. At the risk of sounding self-serving (I am, after all, a real estate appraiser), how about getting a certified appraisal by an experienced, professional appraiser whom everybody was so anxious to circumvent because they were too expensive or too slow? The industry needs to get back to basics before it will rebound and gain back the confidence that is needed to make the markets work in an efficient manner.

Third, put a stop to toxic loans such as the "Option-Arm." These loans bury borrowers much like credit-card debt. Allow a borrower to make a minimum payment that doesn't cover the interest and principle payment and they will do just that.

Fourth, who the heck is originating this loan that an investor is considering purchasing- a mortgage broker working totally on commission that gets paid only if the deal closes? Maybe the originator is a mortgage division of a builder or developer whose main function is to close the loan so that the builder can pay off his construction loan and bank a tidy profit? Maybe it's a mortgage division of a realty company that packages the loan on a transaction that their real estate office put together? No, I think investors want to buy a loan from someone that is looking out for their interest for a change, including performing "due diligence" when it comes to underwriting the loan to make sure that the appraisal is bonafide and that the appraiser is protected by a "firewall" from any lender or broker influence. Investors would like to know that the borrowers actually make the income stated on the application, and that the assets listed on the loan application actually exist and are not just a loan from someone to "beef up" the balance sheet. The investor would like to be reassured that someone besides the investor is putting cash into the deal, and that the entity that is funding this mortgage has the financial strength to repurchase this loan if everything is *not* as stated. "Gee, isn't that the old way?" you ask. Yes, it is. I am reminded of the old Paine Webber commercial where the famous actor John Houseman says, "At Paine Webber, we make our money the old fashioned way- we earn it."

It's not going to be easy to bring back confidence to the mortgage marketplace, but addressing these issues would be a great start. Once we have transparency in the industry, investors will see what they are actually being asked to invest in. As we now know, getting a rubber-stamped rating of "Investor-Grade" by a rating agency is no longer a stamp of approval.

We also need to look at, not only the licensing of mortgage brokers, but underwriters as well. As long as an underwriter makes the decision to fund a particular loan or not fund the loan, they should be made responsible for their decisions that are similar to an appraiser making a judgment about the value of a property. If they have "skin in the game," like a license, they have something to lose. I promise you the relationship that this would develop with the appraisal community would be a lot less adversarial in nature.

A few of the alternatives to the current laws and regulations currently under implementation that the Alabama Real Estate Appraisers Board recommends to their Attorney General, are:

> Mortgage professionals should be licensed and/ or certified and mortgage professionals should sign a certification that they did not influence the appraisal process in any way (this certification would hold mortgage professionals civilly and criminally responsible.

The Builders

Years ago, Gary M., who was my boss at The Colwell Company in Los Angeles in the 1970s, left the company to work for his father, a mid-sized builder and developer in Los Angeles and San Bernardino Counties. In those days, a mid-sized builder would obtain construction financing from a lender or bank and proceed to construct the off-site improvements such as streets, walkways, underground utilities, etc. After subdividing the tract, the builder would begin to construct the framing of the structures, then move on to the electrical, plumbing, and so on until the homes were ready for occupancy.

At some point (normally before construction was started and prior to any kind of loan commitment), the construction financing lender would send out an appraiser who would appraise not only the finished product, but also perform some sort of feasibility study or analyze the viability of the project. This would normally include an analysis of competing projects and their absorption rates.

Over the years, I performed some of these studies myself. I remember a young builder came to The Colwell Company with an idea for a small subdivision of only four or five homes in the Big Bear area of the San Bernardino Mountains. The floor plans were adequate enough, as were the amenities, but they were to be situated so close together that the occupants couldn't help but look at each other through the windows, as they were only three feet away from the adjoining home.

I wrote a report stating that if they omitted one house, the homes would be far apart enough to give each one some privacy. Although this would cut down on the builders overall profits, it would make the project a lot more marketable. The Colwell Company went with my recommendation and the builder agreed to the terms. The loan was made; the builder built out the homes, sold them, and made a profit.

About the same time during the 1970s, I was sent out to Palm Springs, California, where a builder was contemplating building out a small tract of homes. I was able to spend a couple of days with my parents, as they had recently moved and retired to Palm Springs to reside in a beautiful country club setting right on the golf course.

During my initial inspection of the subdivision, I observed the off-sites (streets, curbs, gutters, etc.) were already installed, but what stood out was that shifting sands covered a number of walks and streets and would continue to shift, depending on the direction and strength of the winds. This turned out to be the remnants of a prior subdivision called "Palm Springs Panorama" that had a nasty reputation from prior years. The entire subdivision was subject to these horrific winds, as it was situated in a wind-belt that was so strong that it could topple big-rig trucks on the nearby freeway. A large number of banks had taken a real beating from this subdivision with a substantial number of these lots being foreclosed on. The Colwell Company decided that, based on my investigation, it would not be one of a large number of these lenders and turned down the builder and his project.

Even in the 1980s and 1990s, we had to perform a type of feasibility study when it came to new construction of condominiums. With newly built condos or condos still under construction, we were often required to complete a FNMA form called "Addendum A," which consisted of a two-page form analyzing not only the subject project, but also nearby competing projects that would be in direct competition to the subject. In this form, we were to discuss factors such as density when compared to other projects in the area from a standpoint of marketability and discuss nearby competition including sales prices, rate of sales, sellout times, etc. We had to describe potential for additional condominium/Planned Unit Development(PUD) units in nearby areas, consider land availability, zoning, utilities, apartments subject to conversion, and my favorite: general comments including any probable changes in the economic base of the neighborhood, which would either favorably or unfavorably affect condo/PUD sales. This could include closure of nearby employment centers, construction of new shopping centers, the over-building of similar type projects, or any other factor that would contribute to a change in the local economy.

Although these factors were asked to be discussed in a form for newly constructed or converted condominiums and Planned Units Developments, these same factors should have been considered when doing appraisals on the many subdivisions built over the past five to eight years in so many locations in our country such as the upper desert and the Inland Empire of San Bernardino, California; areas in West Contra Costa County in Northern California such as Antioch, Brentwood, and Fairfield; and the Central Valley cities of Stockton, Manteca, and Tracy. Then there is Las Vegas, Nevada, and, of course, numerous areas in Florida and Arizona.

On a recent drive to Southern California traveling on Highway 395 south of Barstow, my wife and I were astonished to see how many subdivisions of tract homes had been built as far as the eye could see near areas like Hesperia and Victorville on what had been, just a few years ago, flat desert land in the middle of nowhere. One thing that was missing was commerce, commonly referred to as "jobs." Where would all of these homeowners work? I pondered this for a few minutes and dug out the old FNMA form #1004, for appraising Single Family Residences, released in 1993. The instructions of factors to discuss about the neighborhood were printed right on the form, stating, "Factors that affect the marketability of the properties in the neighborhood are proximity to employment and amenities, employment stability, appeal to market, etc." I compared this to a replacement form #1004 released in March of 2005 and was reminded that this whole notion of employment stability and proximity had been removed from the form.

I love the internet with so much data at your fingertips! I went on the Web and found a web site for the City of Hesperia. What I found seemed to confirm what my wife and I saw during our trip through Hesperia. Now, mind you, this "Inland Empire" area of San Bernardino is one of several "Ground Zeros" when it comes to what has become known as "The Sub-prime Meltdown." According to the City documents:

> As of October 9, 2008, 6.1 percent of all homes in San Bernardino County were involved in the foreclosure process at one of the three major stages (NOD, NOTS, or REO) and 3.2 percent of homes were bank-owned (REOs). In comparison, 10.9 percent of homes in Hesperia were, at some point, in the foreclosure process, and 5.9 percent were bank-owners. Hesperia has the fourth-highest foreclosure rate in San Bernardino County and is experiencing foreclosures at a rate significantly higher than the county-wide average.

The unemployment rate, as of June 2008, was 10.2 Percent in Hesperia. I am sure it is higher now and soon to be a lot worse. The estimated foreclosure and abandonment risk score (calculated by HUD, on a scale of one to ten, with ten being the highest risk) for Hesperia ranges from three to ten, with the vast majority of the City scoring a nine or ten.

The City of Hesperia is seeking federal aid to help with the problem in the form of funds to acquire REOs and turn around and sell them as low-income housing. According to their web site:

The City of Hesperia has completed a Neighborhood Stabilization Program (NSP) Substantial Amendment to its fiscal year 2007–08 Consolidated Annual Action Plan and submitted it to the U.S. Department of Housing and Urban Development (HUD) on November 19, 2008. The Substantial Amendment concerns the use of NSP grant funds in the amount of $4,590,719 to be received from HUD. The Neighborhood Stabilization Program provides emergency assistance for the redevelopment of abandoned and foreclosed residential properties as part of the Housing and Economic Recovery Act, adopted into law on July 30, 2008. Eligible activities include financing mechanisms for purchase of foreclosed homes, purchase and rehabilitation of foreclosed or abandoned homes, land banks for foreclosed homes, demolition of blighted structures, and redevelopment of demolished or vacant property.

I guess what disturbs me the most is the unwillingness of so many people, in so many aspects of the real estate industry, to take responsibility for the current financial calamity. This includes regulators and those charged with oversight, credit rating companies, builders, real estate agents, borrowers … The list goes on. Where is the accountability?

Both Fannie Mae and Freddie Mac have recently come up with a new appraisal addendum called Fannie Mae Form #1004MC (Freddie Mac Form #71), dated November, 2008. I believe this is based on a former World Savings addendum that analyzes neighborhood trends with respect to inventory (properties currently on the market), sales, absorption times, median prices, etc. It also looks at marketing times, foreclosures in the market area and analyzes pending sales, expired listings, and withdrawn listings. This, I believe, is a step in the right direction. Of course, it hinges on the person that fills out the data as to its effectiveness.

How can builders keep buying up cheap land in the middle of nowhere, selling the homes with no money down, packaging and selling the loans off, and keep building going, unchecked? This is happening all over the country. A recent AP article sums up a building disaster in Elim Valley, Utah, where nearly four square miles of red-rock desert has been laid out with roads, utilities, sidewalks, and streetlights. Approval has been granted for as many as 10,423 homes, but not one house can be found. The Arkansas bank that initially financed the development has collapsed and has been taken over by the government.

I remember asking Gary M. what his dad did when times got slow in the building business back in the 1970s. He replied that his father would go "on vacation" for a few years until things got better. He would "make hay" when the business was there and coast when it wasn't.

Contrast that with the developer in Elim Valley who got into the real estate game at the peak of the boom in 2006 and expects to build his way out of a down cycle. Excuse me for saying this, but building your way out of a down cycle is like doubling down your bets in Las Vegas, trying to catch up. The house always has more money than you do. You can't win.

According to the AP article, "Walker (the developer) says he needs new loans and buyers to step forward now, before creditors take over." I don't want to be the one to tell him he's in for a long wait, but...

Let me go on record here—I am against builders and development companies having a mortgage division or interest in a mortgage company. Builders packaging the loans of their own customers and funding them through wholesale lenders is such an obvious conflict of interest. Do you think the appraisals will hit the sales prices? Do you think that the appraisers that are performing the reports for these loans will mention that dreaded term "over-built" in their reports? Not likely.

I also don't like the idea of a builder bailout from Washington. The whole development business is based on risk vs. reward. They take the risk, they receive the rewards. It's not, "the taxpayers take the risk, and the developers get the reward." This whole notion of a builder "tax refund" from up to five prior, profitable years to be offset by current losses also annoys me. It's nothing more than a bailout. Next we will be hearing from the oil companies because their profits are down or they need assistance cleaning up an oil spill.

The Good Old Days

Maybe I'm just a sentimental old fool, but I reflect a lot on the old days. A lot of old cliché's come to mind, particularly this one from G. Santayana: "Those who cannot remember the past are condemned to repeat it."

When I think about the current financial crisis, I ponder the way it used to be when I entered the business in the 1970s. Take, for example, the recent lack of liquidity by the banks, mortgage companies, the secondary market, and Wall Street firms and their inability to provide financing for real estate related transactions in any substantial way. Everyone seems to be panicked by this current situation. However, in the late 1970s, I remember most banks and S & L's stopped lending and available credit dried up also. I reflect back and it started with non-owner occupied properties. I was selling real estate at the time and I was trying to put a client into a house that bordered his ranch. He was trying to acquire adjacent properties as they became available to use as "bunk houses" for his ranch-hands. Although his plans included his personal use and use by his employees, these transactions were regarded as "non-owner occupied" loans and we were unable to located financing for the purchase.

Next to go was "owner occupied" financing. When lenders stopped making these types of loans, the real estate business came to a screeching halt, much like today. I also remember that just prior to this previous credit crisis, the home market in California had just gone through a "bubble" period, also much like the recent bubble of 2004–2007. The main difference back then was real estate was viewed as a "hard asset" (as was gold and other precious metals, art, and collectables) and was considered a good hedge against inflation, which, by 1979, was in double digits.

When appraising real estate in the early 1970s, we used to adjust the comparable sales for time using an annual appreciation rate of 5–6 percent. If a comparable sale sold two months ago, we would adjust it 1 percent for time and this would consequently raise our opinion of value for the subject property by that amount to reflect this appreciation. From a practical standpoint, what this meant was that if you purchased a home for $50,000 and suddenly needed to sell it, you would have to wait about a year to a year and a half to recoup all of your investment because it will cost you approximately 9 percent to sell the property including sales commission and closing costs. This 5–6 percent appreciation rate was also higher than the inflation rate for any one of the prior twenty years and meant that your asset was always growing. I don't think many people thought of their homes as retirement nest-eggs, sources of college funds, or ATMs to fund their insatiable consumer-based thirst for gadgets, automobiles, and flat-panel televisions, costing thousands of dollars.

Another factor people considered when purchasing a property in the old days was debt reduction. This was part of the equation, even when purchasing rental properties. The thought of tenants paying off your mortgage was an exciting prospect. Do you remember hearing of "mortgage-burning parties?" I haven't heard of others saying anything about debt reduction for years. Most homeowners over the past fifteen years have been caught up in this cycle of refinancing over and over again. Most of this is to take advantage of lower rates, although a substantial number of people were taking cash out to finance home improvements, cars, televisions, or just pay bills. I would inspect some homes over and over again as the borrowers continued to refinance and add more debt. Some properties I know I have inspected seven or eight times over the years.

These lower rates are sure tempting, but I can't help but think that they will never be paid off! There is so much debt that I can't see how it will ever be paid off without some kind of legal discharge such as bankruptcy. So many borrowers are "underwater" on these home loans.

It's not just homeowners and credit card holders, either. Look at the massive amount of debt being accumulated by the federal government, state governments, and local municipalities. The national debt, as of July 2010, stands at $13,189,319,098,441.58 or $42,724.01 per citizen. It grows at the rate of more than $4.12 billion per day!

According to Federalbudget.com:

> In Fiscal Year 2008, the U. S. Government spent
> $412 billion of your money on interest payments* to
> the holders of the National Debt. Compare that to
> NASA at $15 Billion, Education at $61 Billion, and
> Department of Transportation at $56 Billion.

Even in my small town of Half Moon Bay, California,
the city council has floated a bond measure to satisfy a
federal judgment by a local developer to the tune of
$18,000,000.00. All this adds to the already existing fiscal
woes. I knew a few years ago we were in real trouble with
the economy when the lady standing in front of me at the
bank paid her house payment on a credit card.

As I sit here and ponder the current credit mess we are
in, I can't help but think that all of these banks, investment
houses, and Wall Street firms that are in such dire straits
brought it upon themselves with all of these exotic mortgage products and creative financial instruments (such as
credit default swaps, CDOs, and others), often using leverage at such ratios as forty to one. How can I sympathize
with borrowers that were putting nothing down (or very
little), borrowing at times in excess of 100 percent, lying
about their incomes and assets, and driving up the price of
real estate to absurd levels? Do we really get smarter and
more efficient as we advance with technology and creative
financial products or do we just get faster at inefficiency
and being more frivolous with our money?

I remember performing appraisals on purchases a few
years ago and the transactions were closing in days, not
months like in the old days. I would always think, *How
fast can these people pack and move, anyway?* The transactions would move so fast that I don't see how anybody

could perform "due diligence." Faster, faster, faster! This is still the case with appraisal turn-around times.

In March, 2009, Bernard Madoff plead guilty to running a $50 billion "Ponzi Scheme" for years in New York. The amazing part of this whole story is the extent of the fraud and how widespread it has become. This makes "Joe the Broker," Benny, and the others I talk about seem like small potatoes.

The lesson here is that we all have to perform our own "due diligence" when it comes to our money. This applies not only to us small investors, but large investors, borrowers, buyers, sellers, pension funds, municipalities, schools, and foundations, as well. It also applies to appraisers.

I don't agree with the recent bailouts being made by the administration and Congress with respect to banks, insurance companies, Wall Street firms, and the auto makers (either directly or the "Cash-For-Clunkers" program). I also don't agree with bailing out borrowers who got in over their heads. Sure, there might be a few cases of predatory lending, but, from my vantage point, most of the abuse came from borrowers, mortgage brokers, real estate lenders, appraisers, and lenders who lied about the financial details of the transaction including fabricated income statements, inflated assets, and the lack of "due diligence." They knew perfectly well what they were doing and I don't think the taxpayer should have to pay for it.

As I stated in a previous chapter, the FBI recently reported over 1,400 cases of real estate and bank fraud under investigation. Are you kidding me? 1,400? If you were to investigate every stated-income loan made in the past five years, you would probably find that most committed fraud of some kind, most of which was of a federal nature. You wouldn't have enough jail cells in America to house them all, assuming convictions, because they would total in the millions.

You could fine the violators to help pay for this mess, but most of them are so underwater on their loans and have such low incomes compared to those claimed in their loan applications that it would probably be like getting blood out of a turnip. Going after mortgage brokers who violated the law seems somewhat futile, as most of them are long out of the business.

I really don't understand why more people didn't see this coming. Markets go up and markets go down. It's a cycle and always has been. I'm reminded of a discussion I had with a real estate broker sometime in 2005–06. I was performing an appraisal on one of his transactions. He claimed to teach real estate at Stanford University in Palo Alto, California. I never verified this, but I do remember what he told me after I told him we were headed for a tremendous correction in the real estate market: "Nonsense. There is too much demand and too little inventory. Real estate will not go down in the foreseeable future." I hope he didn't tell his clients that.

The IVPI Proposal and the Appraisers Code of Conduct

I have made a substantial number of criticisms about the appraisal industry and how it interacts with the lending and real estate industries and, in my humble opinion, all rightfully so. What I am now going to try to furnish is a remedy or fix to these vast number of problems.

First, I am not clever enough to come up with this solution on my own but I was lucky enough to come across a brilliant plan developed by a Mr. George W. Dodd, SRA of Ashland, VA, and Ms. Pamela Crowley of Florida, both practicing appraisers.

This Dodd/Crowley IVPI proposal offers an alternative to the IVPI proposal or HVCC (Home Valuation Code of Conduct) agreed to prior to the governments take-over of the GSEs (government sponsored enterprises) and implemented on May 1, 2009 between New

York State Attorney General Andrew Cuomo and the
GSEs, Fannie Mae and Freddie Mac. This was the same
HVCC that so many states and appraisers disapprove of.

The new agreements were among Fannie Mae, Freddie Mac, the Office of Federal Housing Enterprise Oversight, and New York Attorney General Andrew Cuomo,
and were designed to establish a new home valuation protection code with new requirements governing appraisal
selection and create an independent organization to
implement and monitor the new appraisal standards. The
new entity, the Independent Valuation Protection Institute (IVPI) was to be funded by Fannie Mae and Freddie
Mac, which were reportedly providing $24 million for the
effort. As of May, 2010, this has all changed. The Federal
Housing Finance Agency (FHFA) is acting as conservator
of Fannie Mae and Freddie Mac as a result of the government takeover of both entities. In a letter dated May 19,
2010, to Attorney General of New York Andrew Cuomo,
the Acting Director of FHFA Edward DeMarco states:

> "The Cooperation Agreements also called for the
> Enterprises to establish and fund an Independent
> Valuation Protection Institute. The Institute was
> to collect and report on complaints regarding
> appraisals. Of course, the plans for the Institute
> and the Enterprises' financial support for it were
> made before FHFA placed the Enterprises into
> conservatorships. In light of the billions of dollars
> in taxpayer funds the Enterprises have drawn since
> entering conservatorships, I cannot, as a conservator,
> justify the Enterprises funding the Institute.
> Therefore, as conservator, I have determined that
> they will not proceed with that portion of the
> Cooperation Agreements."

Cuomo, Fannie Mae, and Freddie Mac did not adequately address the issue of AMCs and their eventual dominance in the industry, as well as other problems in the industry. Hopefully, someone in Washington will see the wisdom of Dodd/Crowley's proposal and again set the machine in motion.

The Dodd/Crowley proposition clearly addresses several of these problems. For instance:

> Establish a non-profit organization to preserve the integrity of the appraisal process:

1. Transparency:

> A. Regulations to protect and not mislead the consumer, promote consumer confidence, as well as promote appraiser independence.
>
> B. Full and accurate accounting to disclose all fees charged by Independent Valuation Protection Institution (IVPI).

2. Funding:

> A. Funded via a surcharge separate from the appraisal fee. The service fee would be charged to the lender at the time of the order. Appraisal fee paid directly to the Appraiser at delivery of completed report.
>
> B. IVPI would be designed to assume many of the regulatory requirements for appraisal review and quality control of lenders utilizing its services.

C. To become self-sustaining within twenty-four (24) months of full operation.

3. Responsibility:

A. Develop a secure system for the ordering and delivery of appraisal services.

B. Develop a fair and impartial system of audit and review.

C. Develop a fair and impartial system of compliance procedures.

D. Develop a transparent compliance and reporting system.

4. Management:

A. Institute a centralized management team to develop and implement plans of IVPI.

B. Develop necessary business systems and infrastructure.

C. Develop regional areas consisting of three and four States.

D. Create State Appraiser and Review Panels based on competency.

E. Select a location for the main office to conduct business.

F. Hire appropriate operating executives, attorneys, accounting, and information systems to conduct business.

5. Oversight:

> A. Create a Board of Directors that includes:
>
> > 1. Consists partly of experts in the fields of real estate finance, loan origination, law enforcement, compliance review and real estate appraisal and valuation.
> >
> > 2. Consists partly of regional/state representatives elected by Appraisal members.
>
> B. Oversight:
>
> > 1. Oversight panel should be organized on a regional level to interface directly with GSE's local offices.
> >
> > 2. Regulatory oversight by the Office of Federal Housing Enterprise Oversight and the New York State Attorney General.

Dodd/Crowley also proposes a clearing-house or "centralized protected repository for appraisal reports." This does several things.

> It protect(s) confidential information gathered from Consumers and Lenders. The Secured Vault holds the actual appraisal report. A register can be accessed via online query by property, appraiser, borrower, date, case number, etc. Multiple appraisals, reviews, and complaints per property will be linked together so that deficiencies can be identified, remediated, and/or referred as per the Home Value Protection Program.

Can you imagine a vault where multiple appraisals on the same property by different appraisers, possibly in the same time period, could be linked for fraud detection? This would remedy an age-old problem of shopping for the highest value. "The Vault will provide the ability to maintain the appraisal reports in an environment that is free from fraud and abuse. It will provide a central location that investors can access to verify authenticity of an appraisal." This will protect the report from tampering(a large concern with respect to final values), detrimental comments about the subject property on the actual report, and forged signatures.

Another goal of the Dodd/Crowley program is to:

Unify appraisal Policies, Guidelines, and Establish a Centralized Ordering System:

1.   Utilize existing software to develop an ordering system, similar to Veteran Administration's TAS (software program).

2.   Appraisers will register their local market areas; rotational appraisal assignments will be based on technical and geographical competency.

3.   Interface With GSEs to update their policies and format them into a simple and easy-to-follow guide. It should be specific with requirements ordered in a numerical sequence.

4.   Assist the GSEs in combining their policies into a single uniform, USPAP

> compliant policy which addresses
> Consumer appraisal portability; publish
> GSEs policies in PDF format.

This sounds like a great system to me. It reminds me of the old rotational system of FHA in the 1970s and 1980s. No one has control or influence over the appraiser selection process. No appraisal staff members, no independent contractor, no AMCs, no mortgage brokers, no bank … no one. The appraisers are selected for their knowledge of geographic market areas and their technical competency and experience. The same appraiser doesn't keep getting assignments just because he can turn around the assignments faster by taking shortcuts or performing incomplete analysis.

This geographical competency issue is, at first glance, an obvious requirement of an appraiser but you would be surprised by some of the appraisals I have reviewed over the years. When I was performing large numbers of reviews for a national bank's "B" and "C" wholesale loan division, I would come across appraisals performed by Southern California appraisers on properties located in Northern California, some of which were remote and not even within close proximity to a major airport. For those that aren't familiar with California, Northern and Southern California are separated by approximately five hundred miles!

There is no conceivable way for an appraiser to travel that distance and still be competitive, much less an expert in that particular market. Interfacing with the GSEs to not only update their policies, but combine all of the policies of all GSEs into a single and compliant appraisal not only cuts down on redundancy between the GSEs, but makes a single appraisal easier to perform and easier to read and review. It's not one set of guidelines for one agency and other guidelines for another.

Another set of Dodd/Crowley guidelines aims to:

Establish and maintain adherence to the Home Valuation Code of Conduct:

1. The approved IVPI (Independent Valuation Protection Institute) appraiser must personally inspect the interior and exterior of the subject property; virtual inspections are not permissible (viewing photo's, video's, etc).

2. Only the IVPI approved appraiser can perform the appraisal, the only exception being a trainee, or their equivalent, working under the IVPI Appraiser's direct, personal supervision. Unapproved appraisers cannot inspect the subject property and sales independently.

3. Responsible for adhering to the current edition of the GSEs appraisal policies.

4. Certifies to GSE policy adherence in the appraisal report.

5. Identifies the client and the client's "target" lender in the appraisal report.

6. Appraisers to add in additional items required in USPAP for Summary Appraisal Reports (i.e., Highest and

Best Use analysis (HBU), exposure time analysis, the reasoning for excluding approaches or methodology that would normally be expected by peers or other lenders, etc.).

7. Appraisers to model their appraisal reports per GSE approved examples to the extent possible within their geographic region. When GSEs provide suggested verbiage, appraisers should use it to the extent it is applicable, etc.

8. Only individual appraisers are approved.

Google Earth and other satellite photography tools are immensely popular, for good reason. They also make great appraisal tools and are very helpful for visualizing entire neighborhoods and any influence that neighboring properties might have on the subject property (i.e. railroad tracks, industrial land uses in the immediate area, freeway influence, etc.). But they are no substitute for an inspection of the subject property, neighborhood, or comparable sales.

It only makes sense that only the IVPI approved appraiser can make the physical inspection and perform the appraisal. However, over the years, this notion has been repeatedly abused. I remember hearing of one instance years ago where an appraiser would arrive at a property with as many as eight to ten assistants, each performing a different function: one or two would measure the structure, one would take the pictures, one would inspect the exterior, one would inspect the interior, another would inspect the comparables, etc. It must have appeared as a circus to the borrower.

Exceptions are made for trainees working directly under the supervision of the IVPI approved appraiser, as should be, but the point is made, in strong language, "Only individual appraisers are approved."

Guidelines for audit, review, guidance, and compliance procedures are all discussed. However, some new ideas are also introduced that deserve mention.

Establish IVPI State Review Panels:

1.   Regional and State Review Staff and qualified Panel Members will be responsible for conducting audits and reviews, investigating complaints, and associated responsibility.

2.   Automatic forensic review on every property where the loan goes into default.

3.   Conduct training and informational seminars for IVPI Panel Members.

4.   Review written Reconsideration of Value requests.

5.   Review GSE appraisal reports of at least 10 percent annually (Home Value Protection Program).

6.   Serve as a resource to panel members for difficult and unusual properties.

7.   Counsel those in need of remedial education.

Having qualified panel members responsible for conducting audits and reviews, as well as investigating complaints along with Regional and State Review Staff, would not only make the job of oversight more efficient, but having Panel Members involved gives the whole appraisal industry a stake in the oversight process. It would ease the burden on the already overworked state appraisal boards that are, in most cases, hopelessly back-logged on complaints and enforcement issues.

The automatic forensic review of any appraisal that results in a default would speed up the process of oversight and start the ball rolling on detection and prosecution of fraud (if a factor). If fraud was deemed a factor, other reports by the offending appraiser could be retrieved from the "Vault" and examined for fraud before an actual default.

Conducting training and informational seminars for IVPI Panel Members would keep every appraiser up-to-date on GSE and USPAP changes in regulations.

As we know, two appraisers could see things slightly different with respect to values. Often times, a party to a transaction would like to get a second opinion or, at least, get the original appraiser to reconsider his or her opinion of value. These written "Reconsideration of Value" requests would be reviewed, as would at least 10 percent of GSE appraisals on an annual basis.

The idea of the IVPI serving as a resource for panel members for difficult and unusual properties is a wonderful idea and is long overdue. Imagine being able to "brainstorm" with peers and panel members about difficult appraisal assignments while leaving our egos at the door. I remember, years ago, looking up some fellow apprais-

ers who were members in an appraisal organization that
I belonged to, trying to get feedback from them on problems I was having at the time with certain clients and the
way I was describing current market conditions. The con-
sensus was that I was on my own. So much for feedback!

How do you qualify to be on the panel? The Dodd/
Crowley proposal looks at that:

Establish IVPI's Open Panel of qualified Appraisers for
GSE appraisals:

1. All Certified and/or Licensed
    Appraisers in good standing are encour-
    aged to apply for panel membership.

2. Disciplinary action within the past three
    (3) years will require a formal review.

3. Successful completion of IVPI online
    GSE's Standards Course and Updates.

4. Maintain adherence to the Home
    Valuation Code of Conduct.

5. Maintain compliance with the USPAP
    and respective and applicable State
    Appraisal Laws.

It's all about competency, transparency, and plain common sense. I can't imagine any ethical appraiser finding
too much fault with respect to their insistence of continuing education and maintaining compliance to USPAP by
Standards courses, updates by the GSEs, and maintaining
adherence to the HVCC. Some, I am sure, are worried

about being left out, but that's the situation we are in now with respect to AMCs, BPOs, etc.

The benefits of their proposal are outlined as:

Benefits:

1.   Restore the Public Trust.

2.   Promote honesty, impartiality, and professional competency in valuation services.

3.   Increase appraisal portability between Consumers, GSE's, Lenders, Independent Mortgage Originators, and other Market Participants.

4.   A protected repository providing security to investors.

5.   Speed and efficiency become integrated with Appraiser Independence and Competency.

6.   Consumer Hotline and Assistance.

7.   Appraiser Hotline and Assistance.

8.   Effective coordination with Government Agencies and GSE's.

9.   Implementation of IVPI's proposal reduces costly redundancies in the system and results in savings to consumers and Lenders.

Since submitting their proposal to FNMA, Freddie Mac, regulators, and Attorney General Andrew Cuomo,

Pamela Crowley says, "We never heard from them again." Crowley pointed out that Cuomo, Fannie, and the others came up with their own version of IVPI, which appears to be a watered down version of the proposal. At first glance, parts of it are even word for word the same, but the spirit of the Dodd/Crowley proposal is gone.

The new proposal even provides for quality control testing:

> The lender agrees that it shall quality control test, by use of retroactive or additional appraisal reports or other appropriate method, a randomly selected 10 percent (or other bonafide statistically significant percentage) of the appraisals or valuations that are used by the lender, including the results of automated models, broker's price opinions, or "desktop" evaluations.

If I am reading this right, an appropriate method of reviewing an appraisal can be an AVM, BPO, or desk review. Why don't we just go to AVMs reviewing an AVM?

Restoring the Public Trust ought to be at the top of everyone's list, including the lenders and GSEs. They have a long way to go to do that, but this is a good start after years of abusing the mortgage system. Like President Obama said in his inauguration speech: "The time has come to set aside childish things."

We need transparency, honesty, and competency, but we also need regulation and enforcement of that regulation. I hope that the Dodd/Crowley proposal (or one very similar to it) will be passed by the administration for the sake of all of us and will provide us with the foundation on which to build a new mortgage and appraisal industry.

What's Next?

As President Obama said in his inaugural address, "the ground has shifted beneath them," and it continues to shift. Every single day, as I write this story, the ground is shifting and the playing field is changing. Some changes are good; some are not so good.

It is very difficult to keep up with it all. However, with a strong sense of purpose and clarity, with transparency and good old horse sense, we can transform this chaos back into the capitalistic envy of the world. We can again win back the public trust in our services and products, but it won't be easy and it won't be overnight.

In this book, I have outlined the deficiencies in the industry as I see them. Some of them are relatively new, and some have been around for a long time. Some are of an easy fix, while others are more complicated and will take more time and thought.

You won't be able to please everyone, but then it shouldn't be about pleasing anyone. It should be about doing the right thing. I am reminded of one of my favorite movie lines from "Silverado," when Danny Glover's character is in the saloon. When asked to leave because of his skin color, he replies calmly and almost to himself, "That ain't right."

And so it has been with financing and real estate since the turn of the Millennium. The extending of credit to borrowers who lie about their incomes and have no "skin in the game." The banks and Wall Street firms leveraging their derivative positions up to forty to one. The credit rating companies that seemingly "rubber-stamped" investment-grade ratings on to what amounted to "junk." The banks that are not only destroying their own balance sheets, but continuing to do so by acquiring other troubled banks (or Wall Street firms) and then act shocked when it is discovered that there are more toxic loans on the books than when they first looked. Then there is the total lack of oversight by the government entities charged with overseeing both the financial system and the insurance companies that insured toxic loans against loss. There is the disgraceful display by large corporations such as AIG, General Motors, and others with their hands out for TARP funds, like so many children waiting for a piece of candy. There are the money and hedge fund managers like Bernie Madoff and others making off with billions of dollars of not only investors funds, but the funds of well-meaning charities and non-profits (several of which Madoff was a board member). Lets not forget the top brass of Satyam, the Indian Company, completely fabricating assets, income, and even employment figures, and the accounting firms that are suppose to be auditing these firms in an unbiased fashion. To all of these entities I say, "That ain't right!"

I know there are literally thousand of appraisers throughout the country that just want to do a good and honest job. They are conscientious and insightful. They continue to broaden their knowledge of the industry in hopes of becoming better and more qualified in this field. The vast majority of them didn't have a hand in our current financial mess but have suffered the most because there was no demand for an honest appraiser.

These individual men and women have no political clout like the National Association of Realtors, National Association of Home Builders, or the National Association of Mortgage Bankers. Yet, they have to go up against these forces when it comes to lobbying Washington to do the right thing.

A note to the lenders: After you finish driving the last of the honest, ethical, and knowledgeable independent appraisers from the industry, what will you be left with when you really need an expert in the field of valuations? Do you really want just a $165.00-per-appraisal AMC appraiser representing your interests on the stand in a courtroom? Or maybe you could just settle for a BPO performed by a salesman? That ought to go over with a jury. No, the use of the AMC has far-reaching effects that you have failed to factor in to your equation. Just like outsourcing, your decision to go after the short-term gain will compromise your long-term goals.

We, as a society, have to learn to revert back to a time when doing the right thing was paramount over the almighty buck, when your word was your bond and a reflection of your inner-self and strong character. Ethics was second nature and not something one simply danced around or professed to have without displaying it.

With the appraisal industry closely controlled by the big banks through their associations with, primarily, First American and its AMCs, the independent appraiser is headed for extinction. Unfortunately, it is this independence that we need the most so that the valuation of property does not go the way of the credit agencies rubber-stamping of AAA ratings on sub-prime loans or derivatives.

When so much is at stake, it would be nice to know that Congress, the regulators, the President, and homeowners everywhere will back us and help us change the system for the public good. Confidence in the markets cannot be restored until they do. But like so many other issues and reforms like health care, education, immigration, energy, and so many others, I can't imagine it happening anytime soon, if at all.

Glossary

A

AMC (Appraisal Management Company)—These are typically large appraisal firms that employ predominantly entry level appraisers or appraisers with limited experience who will perform appraisals cheaply for access to appraisal business.

Appraiser—This is a person who estimates the value of an asset, usually real estate, for mortgage purposes.

Appraisal Institute—An international association of professional appraisers formed after the merger of the Society of Real Estate Appraisers and the American Institute of Real Estate Appraisers in 1991. The Institute was formerly part of the National Association of Realtors.

Appraisal Subcommittee (ASC)—was set up to consist of designees of the heads of the Federal financial institutions regulatory agencies. It was also established to adopt appraisal standards for real estate appraisal and enable states to form regulatory agencies to oversee the certification and licensing of individuals who are qualified to perform appraisals on federally related transactions. The ASC was also charged with maintaining a national registry of State certified and licensed appraisers who are eligible to perform appraisals in federally related transactions.

Approved Appraiser List—A list primarily maintained by a lender that is comprised of appraisers that have been screened for competency and, hopefully, ethical behavior.

Arthur Anderson—The large accounting firm that was brought down by the Enron fiasco.

AVM (Automated Valuation Model)—A computer generated valuation product designed to speed up the process of determining value and lowering costs.

B

Benny, George—A real estate developer in the San Francisco Bay Area who was charged and convicted of fraud and racketeering in the early 1980s.

Black Panther Party—The Black Panther Party was an African-American organization established in the 1960s that achieved national and international fame through their deep involvement in the Black Power movement. It was founded in Oakland, California, by Bobby Seale and Huey P. Newton

Broker Price Opinion (BPO)—BPOs are prepared by real estate brokers or salesmen and not by licensed or certified appraisers. In fact, they cannot be performed by appraisers because they would violate guidelines set by the

Uniform Standards of Professional Appraisal Practice or USPAP.

Buyer Broker Agreement—An agreement between the buyer of real estate and a broker that represents that buyer on an exclusive basis and not the seller.

C

Carolands—The Carolands Chateau is a 65,000 square foot mansion in Hillsborough, California that is considered a masterpiece of American Renaissance and Beaux-Arts design and is listed on both the California Historical Landmark Register and the National Register of Historic Places. The residence was built by Harriet Pullman Carolan, (born in 1869), the daughter of George Pullman, the 19th century American industrialist who created the Pullman Palace railway car. At one time, convicted racketeer George Benny owned the home and it was later the scene of a rape and homicide.

Certified Appraiser—An appraiser who is certified by the state in which he/she performs appraisals after completing both educational and experience requirements set by the state. The certified appraiser has more experience and education than a licensed appraiser and is able to perform more complex assignments.

Christensen, Dewayne—Dr. Dewayne Christensen, a dentist-turned-savings-and-loan-executive in Southern California, who headed up the North America Savings in Anaheim. He steered the Savings & Loan into development of condominium projects throughout the state in the "go-go" years of the 1980s. He reportedly committed suicide by driving his car into a concrete freeway abutment as the regulators were on their way to close his institution.

Colwell Company, The—A mortgage banker listed on the American Stock Exchange located in Los Angeles during the 1970s. It was acquired by the Baldwin Piano Company at some point and now appears to be long gone.

Comparables (sales)—The most recent, similar type properties used as a basis for comparison in an appraisal.

Comp Check—Typically, a request made by a mortgage broker to the appraiser to try to estimate what the appraised value will be if the appraisal is performed. What this amounts to is an implied opinion of value. It is illegal for a licensed or certified appraiser to arrive at a "predetermined" value. This means an appraiser cannot value a property without inspecting it, gathering and analyzing sufficient market data, and arriving at a conclusion of value that is reasonable.

Compton, CA—A city in southern Los Angeles County, California, that is situated southeast of downtown Los Angeles. The city had a reputation of being one of the most dangerous cities in the United States. It has, however, improved over the past years due primarily to the influx of new home buyers attracted to the low prices of real estate.

Conditions—A request typically made by an underwriter to an appraiser asking for a mistake to be corrected, additional support for a conclusion, such as supplying additional comparable sales, or additional comments to elaborate on comments made in the report. These conditions normally must be addressed before the loan is funded.

Countrywide Financial—Up until the credit crisis, Countrywide was one of the largest mortgage companies in the country. Countrywide was founded in 1969 by David S. Loeb and Angelo Mozilo. The company faltered in the credit meltdown and, on January 11, 2008, Bank of America announced it had agreed to buy Countrywide for $4 billion in an all-stock transaction

Credit rating agency (CRA)—A company that assigns credit ratings for issuers of certain types of debt obligations as well as the debt instruments themselves. These include mortgage-backed securities and mortgage-backed bonds. In most cases, the issuers of securities are companies, special purpose entities, state and local municipalities, and non-profit organizations issuing debt-like securities that can be traded on a secondary market. The rating agencies look at the insurer's ability to pay back the loan. The rating will influence the interest rate of the instrument indicating how much risk is associated with the investment. The three biggest agencies are Moody's, Standard & Poor's, and Fitch.

Cuomo, Andrew—Andrew Mark Cuomo is the New York State Attorney General and son of former New York Governor Mario Cuomo. Previously he was the Secretary of Housing and Urban Development under President Bill Clinton between 1997 and 2001. He is responsible for the HVCC (Home Valuation Code of Conduct) agreement between his office and both Fannie Mae and Freddie Mac.

D

Deed of Trust—A document in certain states where a specific financial interest in the title to real property is transferred to a trustee, who holds it as security for a loan between two other parties. When the loan is fully paid, the monetary claim on the title is transferred to the borrower by re-conveyance to release the debt obligation. In other states, a similar instrument is known as a mortgage.

Desktop Underwriter—A software program of Fannie Mae that helps automate the loan origination process, helps take the guesswork out of underwriting, and reportedly reduces costs. Lenders can process mortgage loan applications in fifteen minutes or less using this software.

Direct Endorsement Program—Direct Endorsement is the mechanism that enables HUD and Federal Housing Administration (FHA)-approved lenders to consider single-family mortgage applications without first submitting paperwork to HUD. This program started in the 1980s and allowed the lender to use their own staff appraisers instead of using the FHA rotational system of assigning assignments to appraisers on the FHA panel. Virtually all single-family FHA mortgage lending is done through Direct Endorsement, which enables an FHA-insured mortgage to be processed as rapidly as other mortgages.

Drive-by appraisal (also known as the FNMA form #2055)—This enables an appraiser to perform an appraisal without actually inspecting the interior of the property. Although it is a modified appraisal report in short form, its recent revisions make it almost as comprehensive as the FNMA form #1004 residential appraisal report (or long form).

Due diligence—Due diligence is a term used for a number of concepts involving either the performance of an investigation of a business or person, or the performance of an act with a certain standard of care. It can be a legal obligation, but the term will more commonly apply to voluntary investigations. A common example of due diligence in various industries is the process through which potential acquirer evaluates a target company or its assets for acquisition. [Wikipedia -Hoskisson, Hitt & Ireland, 2004, Competing for Advantage, p.251]

Duplex—Typically, a two unit building consisting of two rental units that is purchased for the income-producing benefits it provides.

E

Eappraisit—A First American Corporation AMC (Appraisal Management Company) that was used by Washington Mutual and was accused by New York Attorney General Andrew Cuomo of colluding with Washington Mutual, one of the nation's largest savings and loan companies, to inflate the values of homes.

Errors & Omissions Insurance—Appraiser E&O insurance covers losses and legal expenses generated by client claims of error, omission, or negligence during the appraisal of a residential or commercial property.

Ethics—Business ethics is a form of applied ethics that examines ethical principles and moral or ethical problems that arise in a business environment. It applies to all aspects of business conduct and is relevant to the conduct of individuals and business organizations as a whole. Businesses can often attain short-term gains by acting in an unethical fashion; however, such behaviors tend to undermine the economy over time. (Wikipedia)

Expert Witness—An expert witness is a witness who has the education, training, skill, or experience in a particular subject and is believed to have knowledge beyond that of the average person and sufficient enough that others may officially (and legally) rely upon the witness' specialized opinion about evidence or facts within the scope of their expertise.

F

FDIC—The Federal Deposit Insurance Corporation is an independent agency created by the Congress (the Glass-Steagall Act of 1933) to maintain stability and public confidence in the nation's financial system by insuring deposits, examining and supervising financial institutions for safety and soundness and consumer protection, and managing receiverships.

FHA (Federal Housing Administration)—The Federal Housing Administration is part of HUD (or the U.S. Department of Housing and Urban Development) that provides mortgage insurance on loans made by FHA-approved lenders throughout the United States and its territories. FHA insures mortgages on single family and multifamily homes including manufactured homes and hospitals. It is the largest insurer of mortgages in the world, insuring over 34 million properties since its inception in 1934.

Federal Home Loan Bank Board—A former independent agency in the executive branch of the federal government that regulated and supervised the savings and loan industry, the Federal Home Loan Banks, the Federal Savings and Loan Insurance Corporation and the Federal Home Loan Mortgage Corporation. The Bank Board was abolished in August 1989 by the Financial Institutions Reform, Recovery and Enforcement Act of 1989 (FIRREA) and its functions transferred to other agencies, including the Office of Thrift Supervision.

Federal Reserve—The Federal Reserve System is the central bank of the United States. It was founded by Congress in 1913 to provide the nation with a safer, more flexible, and more stable monetary and financial system. Over the years, its role in banking and the economy has expanded. Today, the Fed's duties fall into four general areas: (1) conducting the nation's monetary policy by influencing the monetary and credit conditions in the economy in pursuit of maximum employment, stable prices, and moderate long-term interest rates, (2) supervising and regulating banking institutions to ensure the safety and soundness of the nation's banking and financial system and to protect the credit rights of consumers, (3) maintaining the stability of the financial system and containing systemic risk that nay arise in financial markets, (4) and providing financial services to depository institutions, the U.S. Government, and foreign official institutions, including playing a major role in operating the nation's payment system. (This definition of the Federal Reserve is taken off the Fed's own web-site. I really do have an issue with #2. If they had been following their own duties as outlined, I honestly don't see how this subprime mess could have happened).

Federal Savings and Loan Insurance Corporation— (FSLIC) administered deposit insurance for savings and

loan institutions. It was abolished in 1989 by the Financial Institutions Reform, Recovery and Enforcement Act
(FIRREA), which passed the responsibility of deposit
insurance to the FDIC. The FSLIC was created as part
of the National Housing Act of 1934 in order to insure
deposits in savings and loans, a year after the FDIC was
created to insure deposits in commercial banks. It was
administered by the Federal Home Loan Bank Board
(FHLBB) until the 1980s when, during the savings and
loan crisis, the FSLIC became insolvent. It was recapital-
ized with taxpayer money several times, with $15 billion
in 1986 and $10.75 billion in 1987. However, by 1989 it was
insolvent and was abolished along with the FHLBB.

Fiduciary—In the California Department of Real
Estate "Real Estate Bulletin (Summer 2007, Pg 1), Wayne
S. Bell, Chief Counsel writes: "Fiduciary duties impose
the highest standard of care, and real estate licensees must
be committed to scrupulously fulfilling those obligations."
Mr. Bell also goes on to say,

> …California law imposes the following fiduciary
> duties on real estate licensees: To exercise the utmost
> honesty, absolute candor, integrity, and unselfishness
> toward the client. This requires that an agent not
> compete with his or her client and act at all times in
> the best interest of his or her client to the exclusion
> of all other interests, including interests that could
> benefit the agents or others. In addition, this requires
> that a licensee refrain from dual representation in a
> real estate sales transaction unless he or she obtains
> the consent of both principals after full disclosure.

FIRREA (Financial Institutions Reform, Recovery and
Enforcement Act of 1989)—FIRREA was signed into law

by President George H. W. Bush in the wake of the savings and loan crisis of the 1980s.

In addition to creating new deposit insurance funds, abolishing existing funds, such as the Federal Savings and Loan Insurance Corporation (FSLIC), moving regulatory authority around (authority from the Federal Home Loan Bank Board (FHLBB) to the Office of Thrift Supervision (OTC)), creating the Resolution Trust Corporation (RTC), establishing new capital reserve requirements, and allowing bank holding companies to acquire thrifts, it also established the Appraisal Subcommittee (ASC).

Finiti—An AMC (Appraisal Management Company), a joint venture of two financial industry leaders: First American Corporation and Citigroup. It was launched in fall 2006.

Firewall—A barrier between two entities meant to discourage obvious conflicts of interest, such as between the loan officer or mortgage broker that is ordering the assignment and the appraiser that is receiving the assignment, the credit rating agency and the client that is being rated.

First American Corporation—The First American Corporation, through its subsidiaries, provides business information and related products and services in the United States. It also operates numerous AMCs (Appraisal Management Companies) in partnership with most of the country's largest lenders.

Fitch—is a credit rating agency and one of the three largest such agencies including Moody's and Standard & Poor's (see credit rating agency).

FNMA (Fannie Mae or Federal National Mortgage Association)—Fannie Mae is a government-sponsored enterprise (GSE) chartered by Congress with a mission to provide liquidity, stability, and affordability to the U.S. housing and mortgage markets.

Rather than making home loans directly to consumers, FNMA works with mortgage bankers, brokers, and other primary mortgage market partners to help ensure they have funds to lend to home buyers at affordable rates. They fund their mortgage investments primarily by issuing debt securities in the domestic and international capital markets.

Fannie Mae was established as a federal agency in 1938, and was chartered by Congress in 1968 as a private shareholder-owned company. On September 6, 2008, Director James Lockhart of the Federal Housing Finance Agency (who is rumored to be stepping down as of the end of August 2009) appointed FHFA as conservator of Fannie Mae. The U.S. Department of the Treasury has agreed to provide up to $200 billion in capital, as needed, to ensure the company continues to provide liquidity to the housing and mortgage markets.

Foreclosure—The legal process by which an owner's right to a property is terminated, usually due to default of a loan or mortgage. It typically involves a forced sale of the property at public auction, with the proceeds being applied to the mortgage debt.

Freddie Mac—Similar to Fannie Mae, Freddie Mac's mission is to provide liquidity, stability, and affordability to the housing market.

Also similar to Fannie Mae, The U.S. Department of the Treasury has agreed to provide capital as needed to ensure the company continues to provide liquidity to the housing and mortgage markets.

G

Golden West (See World Savings)

Great Depression—The Great Depression was a worldwide economic downturn and the most severe economic depression in the 20th century. It began in 1929 with the stock market crash of October 29, 1929, known as Black Tuesday, although the great meltdown was actual spread over four days and not just the one.

On September 3, 1929, the Dow Jones Industrial Average reached a record high of 381.2. At the end of the market day on Thursday, October 24, the market was at 299.5—a 21 percent decline from the high. On this day the market fell thirty-three points—a drop of 9 percent—on trading that was approximately three times the normal daily volume for the first nine months of the year.

The October 1929 crash came during a period of declining real estate values in the United States (which peaked in 1925) near the beginning of a chain of events that led to the Great Depression, a period of economic decline in the industrialized nations.

The depression had devastating effects in virtually every country. International trade plunged by half to two-thirds, as did personal income, tax revenue, prices and profits. Farming and rural areas suffered as crop prices fell by approximately 60 percent.

Per Wikipedia:

> The government and business actually spent more in the first half of 1930 than in the corresponding period of the previous year. But consumers, many of

whom had suffered severe losses in the stock market the previous year, cut back their expenditures by ten percent, and a severe drought ravaged the agricultural heartland of the United States, beginning in the summer of 1930. In early 1930, credit was ample and available at low rates, but people were reluctant to add new debt by borrowing. By May 1930, auto sales had declined to below the levels of 1928. Prices in general began to decline, but wages held steady in 1930, then began to drop in 1931. Conditions were worse in farming areas, where commodity prices plunged, and in mining and logging areas, where unemployment was high and there were few other jobs. Frantic attempts to shore up the economies of individual nations through protectionist policies, such as the 1930 U.S. Smoot-Hawley Tariff Act and retaliatory tariffs in other countries, exacerbated the collapse in global trade. By late in 1930, a steady decline set in which reached bottom by March 1933.

Sound familiar?

Greenspan, Alan—Chairman of the Federal Reserve, and one of the most powerful financial men in America, from 1987 until his retirement in 2006. He attended New York University and then became head of the consulting firm, Townsend-Greenspan & Co., in New York, in 1954.

By the 1970s he was advising presidents Richard Nixon and Gerald Ford, and in 1987 he was named Chairman of the Board of Governors for the Federal Reserve System. Greenspan held the post under presidents Ronald Reagan, George HW Bush, Bill Clinton, and George W. Bush. As chairman, Greenspan was largely responsible for directing U.S. national monetary policy; he is often credited with keeping inflation at historically low levels but is sometimes criticized for the "boom-and-bust" nature of the economy in the so-called "dot-com" era of the 1990s. He stepped down from the post on 31 January 2006, and was succeeded by former Princeton economics department chair Ben Bernanke.

GSE (Government-Sponsored Enterprise)—See Fannie Mae and Freddie Mac

H

Hard Money Lender—Hard money lenders often make loans conventional lenders will not touch because the borrower is not as creditworthy as a prime borrower due to poor credit history, inability to prove income, or the self-employed. The hard money lender typically looks at the collateral and its valuation as the deciding factor in making the loan. Interest rates are typically higher than conventional loans due to the risk involved. The defaults are normally higher with this type of borrower. Although sometimes frowned upon, there is a ready market for these types of borrowers and lenders. Over the past several years, these less-than-prime borrowers (sub-prime) had easy access to conventional funds to the detriment of the banking system.

Hesperia, California—The City of Hesperia is located in the Mojave Desert fifteen miles north of San Bernardino on Highway 395, a busy artery from San Bernardino to Barstow and ten on to Las Vegas. The locals refer to the surrounding area as the High Desert. As of the 2000 census, the city had a total population of 62,582. In 2006, the Hesperia municipal government estimated the population at 80,000.

Highest & Best Use—A real estate appraisal term describing the theory that every parcel of land has a potential use (although it may not be its present use) representing its highest present value based on the probable and legal use that produces the greatest net return. For example, an older home on property that is zoned commercial would be appraised as commercial property, not residential property, assuming the commercial valuation is higher.

Hillsborough, California—An incorporated town in the San Francisco Bay Area in California. Hillsborough is one of the wealthiest places in America and has the highest income of places in America with populations of at least 10,000 per Wikipedia. It is located seventeen miles south of San Francisco on the San Francisco Peninsula. The landscape is dominated by large homes; the city enforces a 2,500-square-foot minimum house size and half-acre minimum lot size to preserve exclusivity. As a result, there are no apartments, condominiums or townhouses in the city limits.

HVCC (Home Valuation Code of Conduct)—This was agreed to prior to the governments take-over of the GSEs. Its implementation was on May 1, 2009.

The new agreements were among Fannie Mae, Freddie Mac, the Office of Federal Housing Enterprise Oversight, and New York Attorney General Andrew Cuomo and were designed to establish a new home valuation protection code with new requirements governing appraisal selection and create an independent organization to implement and monitor the new appraisal standards. The new entity, the Independent Valuation Protection Institute (IVPI) was to be funded by Fannie Mae and Freddie

Mac, by providing $24 million for the effort. This plan has since been scrapped as a result of both FNMA and Freddie Mac being placed under the control of a conservator. A number of groups and state regulatory agencies have come out against the HVCC but we will just have to wait and see if it is challenged in the courts.

I

IndyMac—IndyMac Bank was founded as Countrywide Mortgage Investment in 1985 by David S. Loeb and Angelo Mozilo as a means of collateralizing Countrywide Financial loans too big to be sold to Freddie Mac and Fannie Mae. In 1997, Countrywide spun off IndyMac as an independent company.

Before its failure, IndyMac Bank was the largest savings and loan association in the Los Angeles area and the seventh largest mortgage originator in the United States. The failure of IndyMac Bank on July 11, 2008, was the fourth largest bank failure in United States history and the second largest failure of a regulated thrift (Wikipedia).

L

Landsafe—A reality services company, founded by Countrywide Financial, offering title services, flood information, and, of course, appraisal management services.

Lazarus, David—Former writer with the San Francisco Chronicle. He is now employed with the Los Angeles Times and is one writer to watch.

Leavenworth Penitentiary, Kansas—The United States Penitentiary at Leavenworth is located in Leavenworth, Kansas. It was formerly a high-security prison and counted high-profile prisoners as "Machine Gun" Kelly, Robert "Birdman of Alcatraz" Stroud, and George "Bugs" Moran as inmates. The USP Leavenworth came into existence through an act of the United States Congress in 1895. It is now an all-male, medium-security facility.

Liar Loans—Loans that were made with little or no documentation or verification of the borrower's income. These were very popular during the late housing boom and the most toxic.

Licensed Appraiser (see Certified Appraiser).

Listing Broker—Normally the real estate broker/agent who is engaged by the seller of a property to market and solicit offers to purchase. In most states, the listing agent (and buyers agent) have a fiduciary relationship with the seller (see buyer broker agreement).

Loan Prospector—Freddie Mac's underwriting software program similar to Fannie Mae's Desktop Underwriter (see Desktop Underwriter).

M

MAI—The designation given by the Appraisal Institute for senior membership that requires rigorous education requirements, extensive specialized appraisal experience, demonstrated appraisal report writing abilities and potentially pass a comprehensive examination. All requirements to obtain the MAI, SRA, or SRPA designations are significantly above the state and federal requirements. The MAI membership designation is held by appraisers who are experienced in the valuation and evaluation of commercial, industrial, residential, and other types of properties, and who advise clients on real estate investment decisions (according to their web-site). Although the MAI designation represents completion of certain classes, demo reports, and testing, it has long stood for "Made as Instructed" by some in the appraisal industry for its "rubber-stamping" of clients wishes when it comes to value.

MLS (Multiple Listing Service)—A data base of both listings of current properties for sale and historical data such as sales of properties, expired listings, cancelled listings, etc. It is not only utilized by real estate agents, but by appraisers, as well. It is highly localized data furnishing appraisers with not only descriptions of properties but information used to analyze market trends.

Moody's—The credit rating agency that assigns risk ratings to mortgage-backed securities, bonds, and derivatives purchased by investors, pension funds, and municipalities (see credit rating agencies).

Mortgage-backed securities—A mortgage-backed security (MBS) is an asset-backed security or debt obligation that represents a claim on the cash flows from mortgage loans, typically from residential real estate loans, although loans on commercial properties may be securitized as well. The mortgage loans are primarily purchased from banks, mortgage companies, and other originators and then assembled into pools. This "pooling" is typically accomplished by GSEs and private entities, such as investment bankers like the now-defunct Lehman Brothers, Bear Sterns, and others.

Mortgage Broker—Typically originates the mortgage loan and funds the loan through one of many sources such as a mortgage banker (with a wholesale credit line), a bank, investment bank, savings and loan, or a GSE. In the past, the broker was responsible for hiring the appraiser to perform the appraisal leading to wide-spread abuse of the system.

N

National Association of Realtors (NAR)—One of the largest and most powerful associations of interest in America that serves the needs of every real estate broker in the country. Few politicians can stand up to the enormous clout that NAR enjoys. David Lereah was Chief Economist for NAR and served as their spokesman and chief cheerleader giving economic forecasts, interest rates predictions, home sales analysis, as well as other policy issues and trends affecting the real estate industry. His book was re-released in February 2006 as "Why the Real Estate Boom Will Not Bust—And How You Can Profit from It," just before the peak of the market.

NASDAQ—When the NASDAQ stock exchange began trading on February 8, 1971, the NASDAQ was the world's first electronic stock market. At first, it was merely a computer bulletin board system and did not actually connect buyers and sellers. The NASDAQ helped lower the spread (the difference between the bid price and the ask price of the stock) but somewhat paradoxically was unpopular among brokerages because they made much of their money on the spread.

NASDAQ was the successor to the over-the-counter (OTC) and the "Curb Exchange" systems of trading. As late as 1987, the NASDAQ exchange was still commonly referred to as the OTC in media and also in the monthly Stock Guides issued by Standard & Poor's Corporation (Wikipedia).

North America Savings—Was founded by Dr. Dewayne Christensen, a dentist turned savings and loan executive in Southern California (Anaheim). He used North America Savings as a development vehicle to develop certain condominium projects he had going in South San Jose and other areas and was on the verge of being shut down by regulators when he allegedly committed suicide.

No-show—Term used to describe the owner or borrower not showing up for a scheduled appointment to appraise the home.

Nepotism—showing favoritism to relatives, often without their merit.

O

Office of Real Estate Appraisers (OREA)—The state agency charged with the over-site of real estate appraisers in the State of California. It has one of the largest rosters of appraisers in the country.

Office of Thrift Supervision—The Office of Thrift Supervision (OTS) is the federal bank regulator and supervisor of an industry of savings associations and their subsidiaries spread across the nation. The OTS also oversees domestic and international activities of the holding companies and affiliates that own these thrift institutions. The OTS is an office within the Department of the Treasury.

Option-ARM loans—An "option ARM" is typically a thirty year ARM that initially offers the borrower four monthly payment options: a specified minimum payment, an interest-only payment, a fifteen-year fully amortizing payment, and a thirty-year fully amortizing payment. These types of loans are also called "pick-a-payment" or "pay-option" ARMs.

Other People's Money (OPM)—Although "Other People's Money" was a 1991 comedy film starring Danny DeVito based on the play of the same name by Jerry Sterner, it is a real estate philosophy of doing business going back decades. Borrower as much as you can, delay payment for services, and bill it in escrow are familiar mantras for real estate agents and real estate investors alike.

P

Palm Springs, California—Palm Springs is a desert city in Riverside County, California, approximately 111 miles east of Los Angeles. It is known for its golf, luxury homes, Hollywood celebrities, and hot weather.

Pasadena Federal Savings and Loan—A former savings and loan active in the 1970's which was eventually taken over by Citibank. It had a reputation of only lending on what it deemed to be prime properties.

Peckham, Robert F.—Was the chief judge of the Northern California Federal District Court from 1976 to 1988. He presided over numerous high-profile court cases including the U.S. vs. George I. Benny case in San Francisco. The federal building in San Jose was named after him after his death in 1993.

Perris, California—Perris is a town in Riverside County, California with a population of approximately

46,600. Back in the 1970s, it was primarily rural spotted with small ranchette-type properties. It has grown exponentially since then and on March 20, 2007(according to Wikipedia), Perris was featured on ABC's *Nightline* news show during its "Realty Check" segment. The story dealt with the rising trend of home foreclosures in Riverside County, and Perris was referred to as the "epicenter."

Promissory note—A written, dated, and signed two-party instrument containing an unconditional promise by the maker to pay a definite sum of money to a payee on demand or at a specified future date. Normally used in the real estate industry as a promissory note secured be a deed of trust or mortgage.

Q

Quantrix—The AMC formed between First American and JP Morgan Chase.

R

Real Estate Owned (REO)—Once real property has been foreclosed on by a mortgage company, bank, or GSE, it becomes a REO or real estate owned.

RELS—The AMC formed between First American and Wells Fargo.

Repurchase Agreement—In the lending community, the repurchase agreement is most often used between a wholesale lender supplying the funds for a mortgage and a mortgage broker or retail lender originating the loan. It can also be used between a wholesale lender or mortgage banker and an investor or GSE. In these instances, it is typically spelled out in the agreement that if the loan defaults due to fraud, faulty appraisal, or other such deficient component, the originating lender must repurchase the loan from the funding lender. This is great in theory and puts the burden of finding an honest and ethical on the originating lender or broker. The problem with this is that the originating lender seldom has the resources to repurchase many loans in the first place. It's like the local roofer making a fifty or seventy-five year guarantee. Do you really expect them to be around if something goes wrong?

Resolution Trust Corporation (RTC)—The Resolution Trust Corporation was a United States Government-owned asset management company charged with liquidating assets (both real estate and loans) from failed savings and loans declared insolvent by the Office of Thrift Supervision, as a consequence of the savings and loan crisis of the 1980s. It also took over the insurance functions of the former Federal Home Loan Bank Board. It was created by the FIRREA, adopted in 1989. In 1995, its duties were transferred to the Savings Association Insurance Fund ("SAIF") of the Federal Deposit Insurance Corporation or FDIC. In 2006, the SAIF and its sister fund for banks (Bank Insurance Fund or "BIF"), also administered by the FDIC, were combined to form the Deposit Insurance Fund ("DIF") under the provisions of the Federal Deposit Insurance Reform Act of 2005 (Wikipedia).

Riverside County, California—Riverside County is located in the southeastern part of California, stretching from Orange County to the Colorado River. Riverside County is part of the Southern California Inland Empire region adjacent to San Bernardino. The county is primarily a desert and includes the desert communities of Palm Springs, Cathedral City, Rancho Mirage, and Palm Desert located in the Coachella Valley.

S

San Francisco Examiner—A former San Francisco newspaper and competitor of the San Francisco Chronicle. The Examiner wrote extensively on the subject of George Benny during his six-month trial.

San Joaquin Valley, California—Is located in central California and includes such cities as Sacramento, Stockton, Merced, Modesto, Fresno, Tracy, and others. It is also known as one of the sub-prime epicenters of the state where building and development continued unabated.

San Jose Mercury News—The South Bay's (San Francisco) daily newspaper located in San Jose, California.

Sandler, Herb & Marion (see World Savings Bank).

Saratoga, California—A Silicon Valley residential neighborhood comprised primarily of high-valued homes and estates near San Jose, California.

Savings & Loan—According to Wikipedia, a Savings and Loan Association (S&L) is a financial institution that specializes in accepting savings deposits and making mortgage and other loans. They are often mutually held meaning that the depositors and borrowers are members with voting rights, and have the ability to direct the financial and managerial goals of the organization(similar to the policyholders of a mutual insurance company). It is possible for an S&L to be a joint stock company and even publicly traded. However, this means that it is no longer

truly an association, and depositors and borrowers no longer have managerial control.

By law, thrifts must have at least 65 percent of their
lending in mortgages and other consumer loans—making them particularly vulnerable to housing downturns
such as the deep one the U.S. has experienced since 2007.
During the Savings and Loan Crisis, from 1986 to 1995,
the number of U.S. federally insured savings and loans in
the United States declined from 3,234 to 1,645. This was
primarily due to unsound real estate lending as a result of
deregulation. The market share of S&Ls for single family
mortgage loans went from 53 percent in 1975 to 30 percent
in 1990

Secondary Market (see FNMA and Freddie Mac).

Selling Broker—The real estate salesman (or broker)
who writes up the offer to purchase a property for a buyer
as contrasted to a listing broker who lists a property for
sale for the seller.

SLA—The Symbionese Liberation Army was an
American self-styled militant group active in the early
1970s in Northern and Southern California. The group
committed bank robberies, murders, and other acts of vio-
lence including the abduction of newspaper heiress Patty
Hearst. Their demise came in a shoot-out with police in a
South Los Angeles neighborhood.

SREA—The Society of Real Estate Appraisers (see
Appraisal Institute).

Standard & Poor's—Standard & Poor's (S&P) is a division of McGraw-Hill that publishes financial research
and analysis on stocks and bonds. It is well known for
its stock market indexes such as the US-based S&P 500.
Standard & Poor's, as a credit rating agency (CRA), issues

credit ratings for the debt of private corporations as well as the debt of municipalities such as state, county, and city debt. S&P rates borrowers on a scale from AAA to D. For some borrowers, S&P may also offer opinions (termed a "credit watch") as to whether it is likely to be upgraded (positive), downgraded (negative) or uncertain (neutral). It is one of three large credit rating companies (the other two being Moody's and Fitch).

Stock Option—An employee stock option is a call option on the common stock of a company, issued as a form of non-cash compensation. They were typically issued at call prices far below the current market price of the stock. These options were extremely popular during the dot.com bubble of 2000–2001 by startup companies with little or no cash flow. Commercial office space in locations such as Menlo Park and Palo Alto often required potential tenants to include stock options of their start-up company in order to lease the space. The employees or recipients of these "bonuses" used their newly created wealth to buy real estate in the area with little regard to true value. This resulted in an escalation of values in Silicon Valley. Unlike the sub-prime era, most of these investors used the cash from exercising their options to put a substantial down payment towards the purchase.

Straw Buyers—A straw buyer is one who typically purchases a property for another. Sometimes the buyer is aware of this fact but often times the straw buyer is unaware that he/she is being used to purchase property. In one case, straw buyers and their loan applications/purchase contracts were fabricated from information filled out on sales questionnaires in the developer's sales office.

Stated Loans (see Liar Loans)

Sub-prime—The name given to loans that fall below the rating of "prime" loans. These loans are in the riskiest category of consumer loans and are typically made at above-market rates to reflect the added risk of loaning to the sub-prime borrower. Sub-prime borrowers often show limited debt experience, excessive debt, a history of missed payments, failures to pay debts, and recorded bankruptcies on their credit reports.

T

Title/Appraisal Vendor Management Association (TAVMA)—According to their Web site: "The Title and Appraisal Vendor Management Association (TAVMA) is a national non-profit trade association of providers and consumers of real estate title reporting, title insurance, appraisal and evaluation, and closing management services. Our core belief is that all settlement service providers should be free to compete on a level playing field and to conduct business based on the normal forces of the competitive marketplace."

Title Company—Title insurance is an indemnity insurance against financial loss from title defects of real property. It protects an owner's or a lender's financial interest in real property against loss due to title defects, liens, or other matters. It will defend against a lawsuit attacking the title or reimburse the insured for the actual monetary loss incurred. Typically, the real property interests insured are fee simple ownership or a mortgage. However, title insurance can be purchased to insure any interest in real property, including easements, leases, or other interests. Most lenders require title insurance as a condition of the loan.

Tranches—A single bond, such as collateralized mortgage obligation (CMO), may be issued with several tranches offering the investor a piece, portion, or slice of a structured financial instrument or pool of instruments. This portion is one of several related securities that are offered at the same time, but have different risks, rewards, and/or maturities. Tranche is a term often used to describe a specific class of bonds within an offering wherein each tranche offers varying degrees of risk to the investor.

U

Underwriter—determines if the risk to a particular borrower is acceptable under certain guidelines or parameters. Most underwriters use the guidelines of both Fannie Mae and Freddie Mac because the secondary market tends to set the standards.

USPAP (Uniform Standards of Professional Appraisal Practice—USPAP was created with the express purpose of promoting and preserving public trust in professional appraisal practice. Congress contributed to USPAP's acceptance by identifying USPAP as the generally recognized standards of practice in the appraisal profession, as did the Executive Branch, Office of Management and Budget (OMB), and private industry groups such as Fannie Mae, Freddie Mac, and others.

W

Wachovia—Wachovia Corporation was originally created by the merger of the Wachovia Corporation and First Union Corporation in 2001. Wachovia later acquired Golden West Financial (World Savings) at the peak of the housing market, which then led to its instability. First Union was considered the acquirer in the transaction with Wachovia, although the transaction was structured as a tax-free union of equals and the combined entity chose to retain the Wachovia name.

Wambaugh, Joseph—A bestselling American writer known for his fictional and non-fictional accounts of police work primarily in the Los Angeles area. Most of his works are based on his many years on the Los Angeles Police force. He was also involved with creating/developing the NBC series Police Story, which ran from 1973 to 1977.

WaMu (Washington Mutual)—Washington Mutual was incorporated as the Washington National Building Loan and Investment Association in 1889 but has undergone numerous name changes since that time. During the 1990s, WaMu acquired such well-known brands as H. F. Ahmanson & Co. (Home Savings of America), Great Western Bank, and Keystone Holdings, Inc. (American Savings Bank) and by acquiring companies including PNC Mortgage, Fleet Mortgage, and Homeside Lending, WaMu became the third-largest mortgage lender in the U.S.

On September 25, 2008, the United States Office of Thrift Supervision (OTS) seized Washington Mutual Bank from Washington Mutual, Inc. and placed it into the receivership of the Federal Deposit Insurance Corporation (FDIC). The OTS took the action due to a bank run on deposits with the withdrawal of $16.4 billion in deposits by customers following a down grading by credit rating agencies. The FDIC sold the banking subsidiaries to JPMorgan Chase. Washington Mutual Bank's closure and receivership is the largest bank failure in American financial history.

WIC (World Independent Contractor)—Independent appraisers contracted by World Savings to perform appraisals primarily on an "overflow" basis as volume of loan originations continued to climb in the early 2002–2006 time frame. These appraisals were performed by non-staff appraisers but reviewed (often times including drive-by reviews) by staff members or appraisers of World.

World Savings Bank—Golden West Financial operated under the name of World Savings and was purchased in 1963 by husband and wife Herbert and Marion Sandler for a reportedly $4 million. The Sandlers built up World Savings into one of the largest savings and loan in the country. By the time Wachovia announced its acquisition in 2006, Golden West had over $125 billion in assets and 11,600 employees. Wachovia agreed to purchase Golden West Financial for a little under $25 billion on May 7, 2006.

The timing couldn't have been better for the Sandlers or worse for Wachovia, who picked up about $122 billion in option-adjustable rate mortgages. The acquisition proved disastrous for Wachovia, due to the sub-prime mortgage crisis. Most people now believe that Wachovia purchased World at the absolute peak of the housing boom and that this is the major factor in bringing down Wachovia.

Wachovia, at the prompting of the U.S. Government, was taken over by Wells Fargo & Co. in December 2008 in order to head off a potential failure.

listen|imagine|view|experience

AUDIO BOOK DOWNLOAD INCLUDED WITH THIS BOOK!

In your hands you hold a complete digital entertainment package. In addition to the paper version, you receive a free download of the audio version of this book. Simply use the code listed below when visiting our website. Once downloaded to your computer, you can listen to the book through your computer s speakers, burn it to an audio CD or save the file to your portable music device (such as Apple s popular iPod) and listen on the go!

How to get your free audio book digital download:

1. Visit www.tatepublishing.com and click on the e|LIVE logo on the home page.
2. Enter the following coupon code:
   8468-be9f-2ee6-13e3-1f5c-e59a-d118-7012
3. Download the audio book from your e|LIVE digital locker and begin enjoying your new digital entertainment package today!